Invested Stayers

Invested Stayers

How Teachers Thrive in Challenging Times

Edited by
Terri L. Rodriguez
Heidi L. Hallman
Kristen Pastore-Capuana

ROWMAN & LITTLEFIELD
Lanham • Boulder • New York • London

Published by Rowman & Littlefield
An imprint of The Rowman & Littlefield Publishing Group, Inc.
4501 Forbes Boulevard, Suite 200, Lanham, Maryland 20706
www.rowman.com

6 Tinworth Street, London SE11 5AL, United Kingdom

Copyright © 2020 by Terri L. Rodriguez, Heidi L. Hallman, and Kristen Pastore-Capuana

All rights reserved. No part of this book may be reproduced in any form or by any electronic or mechanical means, including information storage and retrieval systems, without written permission from the publisher, except by a reviewer who may quote passages in a review.

British Library Cataloguing in Publication Information Available

Library of Congress Cataloging-in-Publication Data

Names: Rodriguez, Terri, 1967–, editor. | Hallman, Heidi L., 1976–, editor. | Pastore-Capuana, Kristen, editor.
Title: Invested stayers : how teachers thrive in challenging times / edited by Terri L. Rodriguez, Heidi L. Hallman, Kristen Pastore-Capuana.
Description: Lanham : Rowman & Littlefield, [2020] | Includes bibliographical references and index. | Summary: "This book features chapters coauthored by PK–12 teachers and postsecondary teacher educators from across the U.S. that reflect how they persist, remain, and thrive in the teaching profession"—Provided by publisher.
Identifiers: LCCN 2020012618 (print) | LCCN 2020012619 (ebook) | ISBN 9781475852073 (cloth) | ISBN 9781475852080 (paperback) | ISBN 9781475852097 (epub)
Subjects: LCSH: Teachers—United States—Attitudes. | Resilience (Personality trait)—United States. | Teachers—Professional relationships—United States. | Culturally relevant pedagogy—United States. | Social justice and education—United States.
Classification: LCC LB1775.2 .I58 2020 (print) | LCC LB1775.2 (ebook) | DDC 371.100973—dc23
LC record available at https://lccn.loc.gov/2020012618
LC ebook record available at https://lccn.loc.gov/2020012619

Contents

Foreword   vii
   Shelbie Witte

Introduction   ix

I: Social Landscapes   1

1 Do More, Think Again, Keep Learning: Advocating for Refugee
and Immigrant English Learners through Social Justice Teaching   3
   Terri L. Rodriguez and Lauren Thoma Ergen

2 Reciprocity for Critically Conscious Teacher Education   15
   Allison J. Spenader and Leah Shepard-Carey

3 Lessons for Special Education Teachers to Persist and Thrive 27
   *Shelley Neilsen Gatti, Martin Odima Jr., Deeqaifrah Hussein,
and L. Lynn Stansberry Brusnahan*

4 Rowing Together in the Same Direction: How Entwined
Symbiosis Empowers Teachers at All Levels to Embrace
Culturally Responsive Teaching   41
   Katharine Covino, Garrett Zecker, and Hannah M. Britten

II: Political Landscapes   53

5 Ongoing Transformation: Exploring the Chronologies of
Becoming a Teacher   55
   Margaret Flynn and Heidi L. Hallman

6 Beyond Reacting: One New Teacher's Reenvisioning of Top-
Down Accountability Initiatives   69
   Meghan A. Kessler and Arpan Patel

7	Growing to Thrive: The Story of Two Colleagues Prospering in an Era of Standards-Based Education *Eric D. Moffa and Toni M. Poling*	81
8	Sustaining Our Voices: Critical Collaboration through English Teacher Communities of Practice *Kristen Pastore-Capuana and Deborah Bertlesman*	93

III: Disciplinary Landscapes — **107**

9	Persisting in Teaching with a New Vision of Science Education *Elizabeth Xeng de los Santos, Candice Guy-Gaytán, and Sylvia Scoggin*	109
10	An Innovative Approach to Improve College Readiness in Mathematics: A Collaborative Project *A. Susan Gay, Christopher W. Carter, and Carrie L. La Voy*	121
11	Using Digital Spaces to Foster and Sustain an Informal Professional Learning Community *Joe O'Brien, Brian Bechard, Kori Green, and Nick Lawrence*	133
12	Hope as the Catalyst to Thrive in the Profession *Elizabeth Yomantas and Sarah Rosenthal*	145

Index — 157

About the Contributors — 159

Foreword

Shelbie Witte

Dear reader, if you're reading this book, you've been drawn to it for a specific reason or set of reasons. Perhaps you were intrigued by the title *Invested Stayers: How Teachers Thrive in Challenging Times* and selected it as a pleasure read, being interested in the topic of teachers and teaching. Maybe you picked up this book in the bookstore or library because of where it is situated, within the sections of education, advocacy, or policy or nestled conveniently within the three. Or conceivably you recognize the editors' names on the cover or spine, or the chapter contributors' names in the table of contents, knowing their impressive and impactful scholarship individually or collectively.

Perhaps you are a preservice teacher candidate, looking for all of the things you can put your hands on to guide you on your journey as a teacher. If so, I hope this book will show you examples of the importance of culturally sustaining pedagogies, social justice and cultural competencies, persistence in advocating for yourself and your students, and examples of teachers who are thriving in the challenging but rewarding profession of teaching.

Maybe you are an invested stayer, an educator who has shown persistence in the face of change and found ways to use these challenges to innovate. You may see a reflection of yourself in these stories, or reflections of colleagues who work alongside you, and find optimism in their successes and their willingness to share transparently how they've met their challenges with fervent tenacity.

It may be that you are an invested leaver, a former educator who left the profession for personal or professional reasons but still feel a connection to the stories of teachers and their experiences. You might have left the classroom out of circumstances beyond your control, or perchance you left as a sign of resistance and advocacy as to no longer entertain the undue pressures and outside influences prevalent in your autonomy and your profession.

For all one knows, you may not consider yourself any of these and instead have come to this collection as an invested lurker with an interest in education and more specifically, teachers. Maybe you are a stakeholder, a policymaker, or someone genuinely curious about the profession of teaching. Maybe you are looking for answers to "What could be so hard about it?" or "Why do teachers get summers off?" You might want to learn more about what you are hearing on the news, at the coffee shop, or at family dinners when folks share their concerns about "schools these days."

I've come to this book as a reader with a combination of the lenses above and with a solemn intention to find examples of "thrive" within these pages to counter the unproductive dystopian narratives of education and teachers. I bring with me to this text experience as an educator of middle school, high school, and college/university undergraduate and graduate students, threads and characteristics of whom I recognize within the stories shared here. I also bring with me a scholarship of teacher advocacy and teacher professional development that shapes my unequivocal belief that positive relationships (teacher to teacher, teacher to stakeholder, teacher to student, student to student) are the common denominator for any effective and sustainable catalytic change within education.

I read these authors to make sense of how we got here, how education and the profession of teaching, in particular, have arrived to a world of landmark changes and catalysts with remarkable influence on what happens in every classroom without much, if any, input from those it most affects. I come to these chapters to remind myself of the investments made in the lives of teachers and students that pay dividends for generations to come.

As you read these stories, I hope you will notice the relationships between the authors of each chapter and consider the strength each draws from the reciprocal mentoring among one another. I hope you also see the strands of social justice work happening at each turn, making sustainable and fundamental changes to the way educators approach students and curriculum. I hope you recognize the consistent struggle to remain an invested stayer and the ways that the impact of the social, political, and disciplinary contexts and demographics of those who remain.

Whatever has brought you here, thank you. I'm so glad you have the opportunity to read this book, too, and to share in the stories of teacher resilience and fortitude, to share in the lessons of sustainability of the teaching profession, and to embrace the opportunities that long-term mentoring relationships provide for all of us.

Introduction

This book features chapters coauthored by PK–12 teachers and teacher educators across the country, and these chapters reflect how the teachers persist and thrive in the teaching profession. Premised on the idea that coauthors are colleagues and mentors to each other, this book conceptualizes contributors as invested stayers. Chapters feature how particular catalysts, or landmark changes in education, have produced growth, agency, and even resistance across the arc of contributors' professional lives.

TEACHER ATTRITION AND RETENTION IN THE UNITED STATES

Public conversations about teaching as a profession continue to be dominated by a narrative of negativity, with portrayals of the complex realities, challenges, and successes of schooling set aside for headlines focused solely on our field's struggle with retention. During the first ten months of 2018, many news outlets featured US Department of Labor data about public educators quitting at an average of eighty-three per ten thousand a month, prompting renewed interest in this phenomenon and perpetuating the narrative of an institution in crisis. Although still lower than the rate for US workers overall, this is the highest rate of exit for public educators since 2001 (Hackman & Morath, 2018).

School districts struggle to find qualified teachers to fill vacancies, and states are changing requirements to allow individuals with little or no university-based teacher preparation to secure temporary teaching jobs or obtain certification through accelerated alternative pathways (Ingersoll et al., 2014). As Darling-Hammond (2000) notes, student achievement is linked to teacher experience and knowledge, leaving students to bear the impact of growing teacher turnover. Simultaneously, many teachers, with the support of unions (most recently in California, Arizona, Colorado, West Virginia, Oklahoma, and Illinois), participated in protests and strikes to advocate for pay increases, secure collective bargaining, and argue for curricular autonomy within a landscape of top-down educational mandates. Some attribute these tensions as additional factors for recent teacher attrition (Zarra, 2018). Day and Gu (2010) state that the highest rates of teacher attrition occur during the first two years on the job, with half of all US public school teachers leaving prior to their fifth year in the classroom (Ingersoll et al., 2014).

Teachers' decision to exit the profession range from a myriad of reasons, such as job satisfaction, feelings of competence/self-efficacy, person-environment fit, demographic and socioeconomic differences between teachers and students, labor markets, lack of administrative support, school contextual factors, and one's experience or teacher preparation pathway (Vagi et al., 2017). Work that features early career teachers' decisions to leave the profession (e.g., Scherff & Daria, 2010) look to teachers' stories of induction as a way to uncover what factors lead to teachers' exits.

When experienced teachers exit, students are frequently taught by less experienced teachers, suggesting an impact on the quality of curriculum and instruction (Fibkins, 2012). This leaves schools to recruit, mentor, and train new teachers, which can disrupt their ability to provide consistent and impactful learning experiences and add a financial burden to districts. Although this issue crosses states, schools that serve economically disadvantaged communities are often affected the most, with consequences that hurt both individual and community progress (Campano et al., 2013).

In recent scholarship, Glazer examines the concept of invested leavers, former teachers who were fully certified before leaving the profession. Glazer's (2018b) concept seeks to understand attrition through a potentially different lens, positing that an invested leaver's exit can be a form of resistance, "a refusal to do the job in certain ways or under certain conditions" (p. 63). In Glazer's study, the teachers' exits were not just about securing a new career because they were not successful in the classroom. Instead, they were conceptualized as an act of resistance to education policies and practices that were not aligned with their own, not simply a by-product of a highly mobile twenty-first-century economy.

Teacher attrition and retention are challenges that require multiple approaches to not only understand the issues but also aid in the creation of solutions. This book draws on work exploring teacher retention and attrition within the context of our ever-changing world, while viewing the concept of resistance through a new lens. By inviting the stories of teachers and teacher educators who have stayed in this field—those we call *invested stayers*—we highlight how these educators cultivate agency as a way to not only sustain their careers but also grow, learn, shift, and hone their craft to provide meaningful learning experiences for students and themselves.

INVESTED STAYERS

Invested stayers are those who demonstrate persistence while not only embracing change but inviting it through inquiry, creativity, and innovation. The term invested stayers is constructed, in part, through Glazer's (2018a, 2018b, 2019) concept of invested leavers. Glazer describes invested leavers as teachers who were fully credentialed and prepared, who made it through the "survival period," who had reached a level of stability and success in the classroom, and who then decided to leave teaching. Invested stayers are those who are very much like Glazer's invested leavers yet have confronted the complicated realities of the profession and have named themselves *stayers*.

We also place the concept of invested stayer in conversation with the literature about teacher resilience. We see distinct differences in how we conceptualize resilience through our notion of invested stayers; however, teacher resilience is almost always conceptualized as an individual experience around the navigation of personal challenges within the classroom and institutional environment (Beltman et al., 2011). We broaden the notion of teacher resilience to encompass the fostering of teacher leadership and voice, the development of professional relationships, and the active promotion of institutional well-being (Margolis, 2008, 2011; Margolis et al., 2014).

The alternative framework that we pose is one that views persistence and thriving as available for those who take advantage of *generative* and *regenerative* possibilities (Margolis, 2008). According to Margolis, generative possibilities include opportunities that sponsor teachers in widening their sphere of influence and collaborating with other professionals. Regenerative opportunities are those that keep teachers excited about teaching. We consider the agency to take advantage of such opportunities as essential for invested stayers who contribute as school leaders.

NARRATIVES OF INVESTED STAYERS

Invested stayers view professional learning as central to resilience and persistence. Rather than a top-down model of professional development often imposed upon them, invested stayers agentively organize and act upon their own interests to drive professional learning (Smith, 2017). A tenet of professional learning focuses on placing learning within a specific, meaningful context and collaborating with a group of professionals as a route to foster new learning.

Invested stayers' narratives give us insight into the catalysts that affect change across schooling contexts and how educators have persisted and thrived in response to change. In this book, we describe *landmark catalysts* as the sites that denote the overarching social, political, and disciplinary conflicts and challenges teachers and teacher educators navigate throughout their professional lives.

This book was imagined as a space for educators to explore the space of the *relational*—the relationship between teacher educators' and teachers' knowledge. Creating a space featuring co-constructed narratives is rare in the education literature, apart from action research (Mills, 2010). For this reason, the book takes an explicit stand for contributors to either co-construct or feature individual narratives alongside each other. We recognize that the spaces in which teachers and teacher educators work are different, with teacher educators often having access to the affordances of higher education, including access to sharing knowledge in scholarly venues.

In this book, we consider what might occur if educators had space and time to write together and reflect on how they've persisted. Would this affect their professional learning in new ways? What if educators had time and space together to make visible the things that sustain them, especially highlighting the role of professional relationships? How might this process impact professional learning?

OVERVIEW OF THE BOOK

The book is organized through exploring educators' persistence in response to landmark catalysts that frame the field today. We name these landscapes as (1) social landscapes, (2) political landscapes, and (3) disciplinary landscapes. Social landscapes consider the cultural and linguistic knowledge and resources of educators, students, and their communities within increasingly globalized contexts and how these affect schooling in the United States. Political landscapes aim to capture the ways in which educators have been increasingly pulled in their teaching careers toward standardized forms of teaching and assessments. Finally, the third section of the book, disciplinary landscapes, discusses how disciplinary innovation can be a prompt for educators' evolving teaching practices.

Part I: Social Landscapes

Academic achievement and resource gaps between students from diverse socioeconomic and demographic backgrounds are well known to be both a historic and persistent problem in US schools (see, e.g., Bound & Turner, 2011; Spatig-Amerikaner, 2012). It is important that schools continue to document achievement and access, particularly in relation to students' and educators' demographic backgrounds. Demographic profiles are based upon socially and often legally constructed categories that include race, socioeconomic status, ethnicity, language, religion, ability, and gender, among others.

Over the past several decades, US schools have been experiencing growth in numbers of PK–12 students who speak a language other than English at home and are foreign-born or first-generation immigrants (Moughamian et al., 2009). More recently, massive population shifts have occurred due to widespread global crises and migrations of people. The size of the global refugee population reached the highest known to date in 2017, with half of all refugees being school-aged children (United Nations High Commissioner for Refugees [UNHCR], 2018 as cited in Wang et al., 2019).

As the racial, ethnic, and linguistic diversity of students in PK–12 schools increases, the teaching force remains predominantly white, Euro-American, and monolingual in English (Taie & Goldring, 2017). This is important to consider because scholars find that these demographic differences between PK–12 students and teachers affect classroom learning experiences (see e.g., Gershenson et al., 2015). The "achievement debt," or gap in academic achievement between students from ethnically, racially, and linguistically diverse communities, continues to accrue (Ladson-Billings, 2006a); National Assessment of Educational Progress [NAEP], 2019). Education disparities are mirrored in socioeconomic disparities that pervade schools and communities and affect access to health care, jobs, and higher education.

Educators' professional knowledge and ability to provide culturally responsive education remains a critical priority (Gagne et al., 2017). Educators need explicit knowledge of the contexts of their students' lives and the sociopolitical forces shaping their experiences. For example, teachers of refugee students need to learn about their students' personal and political histories as well as their specialized education needs (Strekalova & Hoot, 2008).

Ladson-Billings (2006b) suggests that how teachers think about social contexts, students, curriculum, and instruction is central to culturally relevant teaching. Although culturally relevant teachers may practice a wide range of methods and instructional strategies, they hold several characteristics in common. The first is a focus on academic achievement, or student learning. The second is cultural competence. Culturally competent teachers help students "recognize and honor their own cultural beliefs and practices while acquiring access to the wider culture" (Ladson-Billings, 2006b, p. 36). Finally, they are socially and politically conscious. They educate themselves about social and political issues within the school and the wider community that affect their students' lives and then incorporate these into their teaching.

Educators featured in Part I of the book identify as culturally relevant teachers who persist and thrive through a continual focus on the social and political contexts of their classrooms and their students' lives. These authors narrate the ways in which they draw upon their own and their students' backgrounds and knowledge to improve academic achievement and students' experiences of school.

In chapter 1: "Do More, Think Again, Keep Learning: Advocating for Refugee and Immigrant English Learners through Social Justice Teaching," Terri L. Rodriguez and Lauren Thoma Ergen reflect on their work as educators committed to socially just pedagogies in support of students with refugee backgrounds. Lauren is a teacher of new-to-country students in a public high school; Terri is her former university instructor and a teacher educator in a small liberal arts college. Together, they share the goal of developing socially just pedagogies that go beyond traditional English as a second language (ESL) and English language arts instructional models.

Chapter 2: "Reciprocity for Critically Conscious Teacher Education," by Allison J. Spenader and Leah Shepard-Carey, explores the reciprocal nature of professional development. The narrative follows Allison's and Leah's evolution as ESL teachers/teacher educators whose praxis takes on new and expanding areas of focus. Their professional relationship is described through the presentation of vignettes that illustrate key moments when they engage in meaningful explorations of critical approaches to teacher education.

In chapter 3: "Lessons for Special Education Teachers to Persist and Thrive," Shelley Neilsen Gatti, Martin Odima Jr., Deeqaifrah Hussein, and L. Lynn Stansberry Brusnahan address the importance of recruiting and retaining special educators of color. The chapter highlights narratives of two teacher leaders, Martin and Deeqaifrah, who thrive because of their relationships with, and connections to, their former mentors and teacher educators, Shelley and Lynn, at the university level.

Chapter 4: "Rowing Together in the Same Direction: How Entwined Symbiosis Empowers Teachers at All Levels to Embrace Culturally Responsive Teaching," by Katharine Covino, Garrett Zecker, and Hannah Mariah Britten, outlines a model for practicing culturally relevant teaching. The authors explore culturally responsive teaching from three distinct yet overlapping perspectives. Together, the three voices make clear that only by rowing together in the same direction can they shelter themselves from the prevailing winds that seek to couple minority status with failure.

Part II: Political Landscapes

High-stakes testing, accountability, and increased assessments in US schools have created new challenges for school administrators, teachers, families, and students (Nichols & Berliner, 2007). With the advent of No Child Left Behind (NCLB), high-stakes tests (standardized tests with stakes attached to them) were implemented in US schools in a business-model fashion; it was argued that such tests would lead to increased efficiency and provide schools with the data needed for improvement (Ravitch, 2009).

NCLB, however, has been met with much criticism since its inception; many scholars (e.g., Au, 2009; Hursh, 2007) claim that one cannot understand the effects of NCLB, the rise of high-stakes testing, and increased school accountability without situating them within the context of neoliberalism. Neoliberal ideology, according to Apple (2006), positions individuals as "autonomous entrepreneurs" who can attend to their own needs, are capable of rationally assessing the costs and benefits of their decisions, and "perceive individuals who do not 'make it' [as having] made poor decisions" (Dawson, 2012, p. 2).

Teachers, by and large, have not been friends of standardized assessments and often possess the intuitive understanding of assessments' misuse in schools and classrooms. Yet teachers understand increased testing as part of the world in which they now live. Educators featured in part II of the book are featured as navigating and persisting in their teaching while also adhering to changing political contexts.

In chapter 5: "Ongoing Transformation: Exploring the Chronologies of Becoming a Teacher," Margaret Flynn and Heidi L. Hallman build upon Britzman's (1991) concept of *chronologies*. Arguing that the process of teachers' evolution throughout their careers is influenced by chronologies, which convey a simultaneity of time, place, events, and the meanings that we give to them (Britzman, 1991, p. 55), Flynn and Hallman trace the chronologies in their own careers as teacher and teacher educator in order to highlight moments where the political dimension of teaching and schooling played a significant role.

Chapter 6: "Beyond Reacting: One New Teacher's Reenvisioning of Top-Down Accountability Initiatives," by Meghan A. Kessler and Arpan Patel, features the effects of top-down educational reform on one beginning teacher, Arpan. Describing these initiatives as framed by restrictive curriculum, overemphasis on testing, and the deprofessionalization of teachers, this chapter locates such reforms as especially commonplace in urban settings that have been subjected to years of slim resource allocation and private-sector influences.

Chapter 7: "Growing to Thrive: The Story of Two Colleagues Prospering in an Era of Standards-Based Education," by Eric D. Moffa and Toni M. Poling, examines the ways that two former high school teacher colleagues thrived in a standards-based educational environment by seeking pathways for professional development and personal growth. These pathways led each colleague toward innovative pedagogies in their disciplines and to take on roles as teacher-leaders.

Chapter 8: "Sustaining Our Voices: Critical Collaboration through English Teacher Communities of Practice," by Kristen Pastore-Capuana and Deb

Bertlesman, discusses how participation in a statewide professional community can sustain teachers' work. Deb, a veteran English teacher, and Kristen, an English teacher educator, feature how the collaboration fostered within this professional network helped Deb advocate for curricula that authentically addressed the needs and interests of her students.

Part III: Disciplinary Landscapes

The twenty-first-century education system, which largely remains a traditional, one-size-fits-all model, is poised for rapid change and innovation within the context of our modern knowledge society. Day's (2001) argument that "teachers are potentially the most important asset in the notion of a learning society" (p. 495) is even more true today. Hargreaves (2003) adds that teachers are poised to participate in the creation of new visions of schooling in the face of a systems that remain "obsessed with imposing and micromanaging curriculum uniformity" (p. 1). The chapters in this section explore how, while traditional structures may remain in place, invested stayers subversively and actively work within and around these structures in transformative ways.

Chapter authors still generally see themselves as residing in a particular disciplinary domain, such as history, English language arts, science, or mathematics, with each domain having unique disciplinary features that make it its own. Nonetheless, many educators view interdisciplinary connections between subject areas and redefine the boundaries and identities of each domain while creating new subjects, programs, and pedagogical approaches. The value shift from content to skills, community, and intellectual and emotional engagement presents new opportunities for interdisciplinary and real-world collaboration.

Another catalyst for disciplinary change is technology's increased implementation. Technology use has continued to rise in schools throughout the past decade, and although most states are now funding student education, in general, at a lesser level than before the recession in 2007 (Leachman & Mai, 2013), Rizzo (2013) notes that more than 37 percent of public schools and at least thirty-three states have schools implementing 1:1 programs.

The third section of the book invites readers to consider how teachers of particular subject areas have held onto a disciplinary common ground despite changes they see in the landscape of what it means to be a teacher today. These educators narrate their experiences with developing new visions for classroom teaching and teacher development across unique contexts and changing discipline methodologies. Together, they argue for the power of collaboration to create spaces for educators to sustain professional identities and advocate for innovative approaches while navigating complex equity issues and curricular mandates.

In chapter 9: "Persisting in Teaching with a New Vision of Science Education," Elizabeth Xeng de los Santos, Candice Guy-Gaytán, and Sylvia Scoggin explore the challenging instructional shifts science teachers and teacher educators make to meaningfully implement the Next Generation Science Standards (NGSS). Discussing how the authors' continually evolving collaboration helped them to persevere in this changing disciplinary shift, Elizabeth, Candice, and Sylvia present a Research-Practice Partnership (RPP) between university researchers and teachers in a large public school district.

Chapter 10: "An Innovative Approach to Improve College Readiness in Mathematics: A Collaborative Project," by A. Susan Gay, Christopher W. Carter, and Carrie L. La Voy, illustrates an innovative partnership between a high school math teacher and two teacher educators created to address the need to better support high school seniors who struggled to succeed in college algebra. The creation of a senior algebra course built on differentiated instruction and individualized, diverse assessments emerged from this collaboration.

In chapter 11: "Using Digital Spaces to Foster and Sustain an Informal Professional Learning Community," Joe O'Brien, Brian Bechard, Kori Green, and Nick Lawrence explore their experiences with a digital social studies classroom and its evolution into a networked public space connecting students and teachers across multiple schools. Exploring concepts surrounding Just War, teachers and students connected and inquired into ethical issues in civics, analyzed primary source texts collaboratively, and tested new digital learning tools.

Finally, chapter 12: "Hope as the Catalyst to Thrive in the Profession," by Elizabeth Yomantas and Sarah Rosenthal, examines how a teacher and teacher educator created a professional development school (PDS) partnership committed to equity and conceptualized as a vehicle to push back against the professional demands and isolation felt by both educators. Foregrounding their partnership in a shared orientation of hope, the authors reenvision teacher education and secondary school relationships through building authentic relationships between school partners, creating a new vision for clinical placements, and nurturing personal and professional identities.

IMAGINING WHAT IS POSSIBLE

Throughout this book, contributors speak about how they persist and thrive within challenging, yet exciting, times marked by landmark catalysts across social, political, and disciplinary landscapes. These authors narrate themselves as invested stayers who invite personal and professional growth through inquiry, creativity, and innovation.

Each chapter offers a response to questions about what might occur if educators had space and time to write together and, more importantly, to reflect on personal and professional growth. Clearly these co-constructed narratives present views of professional learning as relational. Coauthors share a dialogic understanding of knowledge (Bakhtin, 1981, 1986) that highlights the reciprocal nature of learning and the power of relational ways of knowing and being.

We were surprised by the hearty response to our call for teachers and teacher educators to reflect on how their relationships sustain them. We were also encouraged. In a world where we often hear about the challenges educators face, we do not often hear from educators themselves about how they have taken agency in their own professional development and lives. Reframing teacher persistence by paying attention to what sustains them and how they thrive, not just what makes them leave the profession, is essential to imagining what is possible.

REFERENCES

Apple, M. W. (2006). Understanding and interrupting neoliberalism and neoconservatism in education. *Pedagogies: An International Journal, 1*, 21–26.

Au, W. (2009). Obama, Where art thou? Hoping for change in U.S. education policy. *Harvard Educational Review, 79*(2), 309–321.

Bakhtin, M. M. (1981). *The dialogic imagination: Four essays*. In M. Holquist (Ed.). Austin: University of Texas Press.

Bakhtin, M. M. (1986). *Speech genres and other late essays*. In C. Emerson & M. Holquist (Eds.) Austin: University of Texas.

Beltman, S., Mansfield, C. F., & Price, A. E. (2011). Thriving not just surviving: A review of research on teacher resilience. *Educational Research Review, 6*(3), 185–207.

Bound, J., & Turner, S. (2011). Dropouts and diplomas: The divergence in collegiate outcomes. In E. A. Hanushek, S. J. Machin, & L. Woessman (Eds.), *Handbook of the economics of education* (Vol. 4, pp. 573–613). Amsterdam: North-Holland.

Britzman, D. P. (1991). *Practice makes practice: A critical study of learning to teach*. Albany, NY: State University of New York Press.

Campano, G., Ghiso, M., & Sánchez, L. (2013). "Nobody Knows the . . . Amount of a Person": Elementary Students Critiquing Dehumanization through Organic Critical Literacies. *Research in the Teaching of English, 48*(1), 98–125. Retrieved January 9, 2020, from www.jstor.org/stable/24398648

Darling-Hammond, L. (2000). Teacher quality and student achievement: A review of state policy evidence. *Educational Policy Analysis Archives, 8*(1). Retrieved January 10, 2020, from http://epaa.asu.edu/epaa/v8n1

Dawson, H. (2012). Teachers' motivation and beliefs in a high-stakes testing context [unpublished dissertation].

Day, C. (2001). Innovative teachers: Promoting lifelong learning for all. In J. C. D. Aspin, M. Hatton, & Y. Sawano (Eds.), *International handbook of lifelong learning* (pp. 473–500). London: Kluwer.

Day, C., & Gu, Q. (2010). *The new lives of teachers*. London: Routledge.

Fibkins, W. L. (2012). *Stopping the brain drain of skilled veteran teachers: Retaining and valuing their hard-won experience*. Lanham, MD: Rowman & Littlefield.

Gagne, A., Schmidt, C., & Markus, P. (2017). Teaching about refugees: Developing culturally responsive educators in contexts of politicised transnationalism. *Intercultural Education, 28*(5), 429–446. doi: 10.1080/14675986.2017.1336409

Gershenson, S., Holt, S. B., & Papageorge, N. W. (2015). "Who believes in me?" The effect of student-teacher demographic match on teacher expectations. Upjohn Institute Working Paper, 15–231. Kalamazoo, MI: W. E. Upjohn Institute for Employment Research. Retrieved December 12, 2019, from http://dx.doi.org/10.17848/wp15-231

Glazer, J. (2018a). Leaving lessons: Learning from the exit decisions of experienced teachers. *Teachers and Teaching, 24*(1), 50–62.

Glazer, J. (2018b). Learning from those who no longer teach: Viewing teacher attrition through a resistance lens. *Teaching and Teacher Education, 74*, 62–71.

Glazer, J. (2019). Training for the Unsustainable: The need to consider attrition in ELA teacher preparation. In H. L. Hallman, K. Pastore-Capuana, & D. L. Pasternak (Eds.), *Possibilities, challenges, and changes in English teacher education: Exploring identity and professionalization.* Lanham, MD: Rowman & Littlefield.

Hackman, M., & Morath, E. (2018). Teachers quit jobs at highest rate on record. *Wall Street Journal.* Retrieved December 29, 2018 from www.wsj.com/articles/teachers-quit-jobs-at-highest-rate-on-record-11545993052

Hargreaves, A. (2003). *Teaching in the knowledge society.* New York, NY: Teachers College Press and Buckingham: Open University Press.

Hursh, D. (2007). Assessing No Child Left Behind and the rise of neoliberal education policies. *American Educational Research Journal, 44*(3), 493–518.

Ingersoll, R., Merrill, L., & May, H. (2014). What are the effects of teacher education and preparation on beginning teacher attrition? Research Report (#RR-82). Philadelphia: Consortium for Policy Research in Education, University of Pennsylvania.

Ladson-Billings, G. (2006a). From the achievement gap to the education debt: Understanding achievement in U.S. schools. *Educational Researcher, (35)*7, 3–12.

Ladson-Billings, G. (2006b). Yes, but how do we do it?: Practicing culturally relevant pedagogy. In J. Landsman & C. W. Lewis (Eds.), *White teachers, diverse classrooms: A guide to building inclusive schools, promoting high expectations, and eliminating racism* (pp. 30–42). Sterling, VA: Stylus.

Leachman, M., & Mai, C. (2013). Most states funding schools less than before recession. Washington, DC: Center on Budget and Policy and Priorities. Retrieved from http:// www.cbpp.org/ files/9-12-13sfp.pdf

Margolis, J. (2008). When teachers face teachers: Listening to the resource "right down the hall." *Teaching Education, 19*(4), 293–310.

Margolis, J. (2011). What will keep today's teachers teaching? Looking for a hook as a new career cycle emerges. *Teachers College Record, 110*(1), 160–194.

Margolis, J., Hodge, A., & Alexandrou, A. (2014). The teacher educator's role in promoting institutional versus individual teacher well-being. *Journal of Education for Teaching, 40*(4), 391–408.

Mills, G. E. (2010). *Action research: A guide for teacher research* (43rd Ed.). Boston: Prentice Hall.

Moughamian, A. C., Rivera, M. O., & Francis, D. J. (2009). *Instructional models and strategies for teaching English language learners.* Portsmouth, NH: RMC Research Corporation, Center on Instruction.

National Assessment of Educational Progress [NAEP] (2019). *NAEP Report Card: 2019 NAEP Mathematics Assessment.* Retrieved December 12, 2019, from https://www.nationsreportcard.gov/highlights/mathematics/2019

Nichols, S. L., & Berliner, D. C. (2007). *Collateral damage: How high stakes testing corrupts America's schools.* Cambridge, MA: Harvard Education Press.

Ravitch, D. (2009). *The death and life of the great American school system: How testing and choice are undermining education* (1st ed.). Philadelphia, PA: Basic Books.

Rizzo, S. K. (2013). *Making the shift: A phenomenological study of teachers' experiences in student-centered, 21st century laptop program* (UMI No. 3562455) [Doctoral dissertation, Nova Southeastern University]. ProQuest Dissertations and Thesis Database.

Scherff, L., & Daria, M. (2010). *Stories from novice teachers: This is induction?* Lanham, MD: Rowman & Littlefield.

Smith, K. (2017). *Teachers as self-directed learners: Active positioning through professional learning.* Singapore: Springer Nature Singapore Pte. Ltd.

Spatig-Amerikaner, A. (2012). Unequal education: Federal loophole enables lower spending on students of color. *Progress 2050: New ideas for a diverse America.* Washington, DC: Center for American Progress. Retrieved December 12, 2019, from https://www.uncf.org/wp-content/uploads/PDFs/UnequalEduation.pdf

Strekalova, E., & Hoot, J. L. (2008). What is special about special needs of refugee children?: Guidelines for teachers. *Multicultural Education, 16*(1), 21–24.

Taie, S., & Goldring, R. (2017). Characteristics of public elementary and secondary school teachers in the United States: Results from the 2015–16 National Teacher and Principal Survey First Look (NCES 2017-072). US Department of Education. Washington, DC: National Center for Education Statistics. Retrieved November 30, 2017 from https://nces.ed.gov/pubsearch/pubsinfo.asp?pubid=2017072

Vagi, R., Pivovarova, M., & Barnard, W. M. (2017). Keeping our Best? A survival analysis examining a measure of preservice teacher quality and teacher attrition. *Journal of Teacher Education, 70*(2), 115–127. https://doi.org/10.1177/0022487117725025

Wang, C. X., Strekalova-Hughes, E., & Cho, H. (2019). Going beyond a single story: Experiences and education of refugee children at home, in school, and in the community. *Journal of Research in Childhood Education, 33*(1), 1–5, doi: 10.1080/02568543.2018.1531670

Zarra, E. J. (2018). *The teacher exodus: Reversing the trend and keeping teachers in the classroom.* Lanham, MD: Rowman & Littlefield.

I

Social Landscapes

Chapter One

Do More, Think Again, Keep Learning

Advocating for Refugee and Immigrant English Learners through Social Justice Teaching

Terri L. Rodriguez and Lauren Thoma Ergen

This chapter features our narratives as English educators committed to social justice–oriented pedagogies. Lauren is an English language arts (ELA) and English as a second language (ESL) teacher in a public high school, and Terri is a former ELA teacher and a teacher educator at a private college. Like many US teachers, we both identify as white, Christian, and native English speakers. We trace the arc of our professional development through being individual teachers in differing roles and contexts, but we are also collaborators in the shared work of supporting K–12 students, particularly those who are English language learners (ELLs) with refugee and immigrant backgrounds.

Personal and professional narratives of identity are important for teachers to generate and consider, especially in their work with students whose backgrounds and experiences differ from their own (Rodriguez & Cho, 2011). Narratives of identity have the power to help teachers critically reflect on their own backgrounds and experiences and how these intersect with their teaching. They allow teachers to construct agentive identities and enact practices that align with being who they say they are (Holland et al., 1998, p. 3).

In this chapter, we narratively reflect on our personal and professional journeys of becoming invested stayers in the field of social justice–oriented teaching. As noted in the introduction, invested stayers are teachers who stay in the field rather than leave, and this persistence is conceptualized as an act of resistance. Teachers who are invested stayers cultivate agency and continue to grow, learn, shift, and hone their craft, and they resist the demoralization that occurs in the face of consistent and pervasive challenges to enact the values that motivate their work. In other words, they refuse to do that which appears to them to be ethically "wrong" in the name of the profession they love (Santoro, 2018). Such teachers embrace and invite change through inquiry, creativity, and innovation.

We first explore how equity literacy and social justice–teaching frameworks guide our teaching. We then narrate the contexts of our daily teaching practice and the personal experiences that propelled us into our teaching careers. Finally, we describe ourselves as invested stayers and discuss our hopes for the future. Ours is a unique shared vision of student advocacy honed through investment—in ourselves, our students, our own professional development, and the development of a professional relationship that continues to sustain us.

EQUITY LITERACY AND SOCIAL JUSTICE TEACHING

Frameworks for conceptualizing equity literacy and social justice teacher education abound. We share a vision of teaching grounded specifically in theories and practices of critical multicultural education (Grant & Sleeter, 2006), culturally relevant teaching (Ladson-Billings, 2005; 2006), and equity literacy (Gorski, 2014; Gorski & Swalwell, 2015; Swalwell, 2013). Although distinct, these approaches are complementary. Taken together, they offer insights into social justice–teachers' ways of "doing" and "being" (Ladson-Billings, 2006, p. 41).

Equity literacy particularly stems from, and embraces, tenets of the other two. It synthesizes goals of multicultural education and culturally relevant teaching while going "beyond" culture to address equity more directly. According to Gorski and Swalwell (2015), a central tenet of equity literacy is that "any meaningful approach to diversity or multiculturalism relies more on teachers' understandings of equity and inequity and of justice and injustice than on their understanding of this or that culture" (p. 36).

Further, in line with Grant and Sleeter (2006), Swalwell (2013) asserts that social justice pedagogy relies on three essential elements: exposing students to multiple perspectives that include the voices of marginalized peoples; a democratic classroom structure that values student voice; and opportunities to participate in project-based learning and community-based social action that addresses issues of injustice (p. 18).

In addition to these elements that highlight how to "do" social justice pedagogy, Swalwell (2013) describes the identity of the "activist ally" teacher as one "intent upon facilitating the development of justice-oriented citizens with a deep understanding of systemic injustices, a sense of agency that is empowered and critically self-reflective, and the ability to mobilize their resources in order to act in concert with others" (p. 108). In summary, we find this *doing* and *being* framework useful in designing curriculum and conceptualizing their work as educators.

LAUREN'S TEACHING STORIES

Lauren holds licensure in secondary communication arts and literature (grades 6–12) and teaching English as a second language (ESL) (grades K–12). She has also earned an MA in teaching English as a second language. She is currently in her seventh year of teaching ELLs who are newcomers to the United States in a mid-sized public high school in the Midwest. In the following narratives, Lauren describes tensions she has encountered in the development of her professional identity as a social justice–oriented ELA/ESL teacher, explores how professional collaborations and relationships with educators like Terri sustain her, and talks about her hopes for herself and her future students.

Being on Rubber Bands

Lauren describes herself as being on rubber-bands between her two "sides"—ELA and English language development (ELD). This space of in-betweenness has brought her back and forth until she has found a more comfortable middle ground. As an undergraduate student, she sought to become an ELA teacher because of her own preference for the subject. She loved artistic writing and reading fiction.

One year into her undergraduate coursework, she opened a door that introduced her to immigrant and refugee students. She began volunteering at Hands Across the World, a local refugee relief organization that provides after-school tutoring for children with refugee backgrounds. She loved working with these students and listening to their stories.

For the rest of her undergraduate degree program, Lauren saw herself as an actor learning two different scripts for two different shows. She was unsure whether she would become an ELA or ELD teacher. During her first year in the classroom, perhaps because she was such a novice teacher, she decided to stick to one script and commit herself to it. She set out in her career teaching refugee newcomers who had little to no proficiency in English. Many of her students had few literacy skills in any language.

Lauren thought this was about as far as she could get from her ELA roots and her love of English literature and creative writing. She didn't see or understand how she could do a good job honoring "both sides" of her teacher preparation. She felt that she had to position herself far out on a spectrum of ELA teaching, between what is often considered basic English language and literacy skill development and teaching communication arts and literature.

Gradually, Lauren has stepped back toward her origins in ELA and her love for teaching literature and writing. This year, for the first time, she has found a space where she can do justice to both of her teaching lenses. She loves sharing her classroom with students who have immigrant and refugee backgrounds and are beginners in their development of English language skills. She advocates for integration of developmentally, linguistically, and culturally appropriate texts to engage emerging readers. In line with Swalwell's (2013) notions of social justice pedagogy, she encourages students to apply their language growth and literary experiences to tangible change they can make in their communities.

Further, she is actively developing her professional toolkit and employing ELD strategies to fulfill ELA standards. One example of an ELD strategy Lauren uses in her classroom is employing all four language domains in any given lesson so that students can capitalize on oral cultural traditions to support literacy development. Her students read, write, speak, and listen in a variety of ways to demonstrate competency in the ELA standards that otherwise focus on one or two language domains.

Making Space to Do More, Think Again, and Keep Learning

Lauren met Terri about eight years ago during her undergraduate work when Terri was a professor of courses in which she was enrolled. Their professional relationship evolved during Lauren's student teaching placement when Terri was her university supervisor, and again as Lauren became an "official" teacher after graduation. Lauren assumed that this teacher-student relationship would diminish with each year after graduation, when the college no longer tied them together. However, she continued to draw on Terri's support more each year in her profession.

Lauren especially channels Terri when decision making. She tries to use philosophies she believes Terri would endorse and practices teaching models she has learned from Terri as a compass to orient herself. Reflecting professionally in light of the theories and practices she encountered in her undergraduate coursework, Lauren identifies opportunities to make space in her classroom to apply social justice pedagogies. As she becomes a more experienced teacher and takes on leadership roles, she gains opportunities to advocate and bring social justice–teaching principles into decisions beyond her classroom.

Lauren credits Terri's continued support as a major factor in not becoming burned out.

Whether catching up over coffee or framing research or pedagogical questions together, Terri, in many ways, challenges Lauren to be an inquisitive problem solver and to take another step in. Over the years, Lauren has felt that wherever she was in her career and education, Terri embraced and valued Lauren's situation.

At the same time, Terri pushes her to do more, think again, and keep learning. Terri often invites Lauren into pedagogical conversations and research projects in ways that enable them both to improve on their teaching practice. Through this relationship, Lauren and Terri both see their careers as engaging, valid, valuable, and sustainable.

Investing in the Future

In considering how she is an invested stayer in the field of education, Lauren thinks about her relationship with education itself. The first thing that comes to mind is a social relationship as a metaphor for her relationship with education. Social relationships that are the most secure and comfortable, to Lauren, are fifty-fifty. Each person invests and receives return on their investment. Certainly, there are times that very meaningful relationships tip to be forty-sixty or even twenty-eighty—when one member of the relationship needs more support and has less to give—but eventually the balance returns.

Like any educator, she gives a lot to the profession and even more to the students. But she gets a lot out of the investment, too. She learns a lot about herself when she learns about her students. She feels valued. At least, she believes what she *does* is valuable. She has found that the more challenging the environment or situation, asking for the biggest investment of emotional and physical energy, the more fulfilling the return.

Lauren would say that her investment in education is selfish. She dwells on the symbiotic relationship. She understands that sometimes she will have to give more and get less, but at those times she believes fully that she is investing in the future. Not simply her future "payback," but the future—everyone's future.

Lauren is not sure that she would recognize herself if she weren't in this field. She considers herself an invested stayer because she does not only self-identify as a teacher when she meets someone new who asks, "So, what do you do for a living?" She self-identifies as an educator in nearly everything she does because the investment pays out in so many wonderful ways that make her whole life, each facet of it, very rich.

TERRI'S TEACHING STORIES

Terri is a former secondary ELA teacher and professor of education at a small, private liberal arts college in the midwestern United States. She has been licensed as an ELA teacher in several different states and worked as a middle and secondary ELA teacher for seven years in both private and public schools. She earned an MEd in secondary English education and a PhD in curriculum and instruction. She has been formally teaching for more than twenty-five years. In the following narratives, Terri describes the lifelong development of her teacher identity, explores how she continues to learn and hone her teaching through ongoing professional relationships with former students like Lauren, and talks about how she frames leaving the secondary classroom as an agentive act of resistance.

Teaching as "Mushfake"

When pressed to tell the story of the development of her teaching identity, Terri explains that she has always been a teacher. At the age of ten, she remembers her two-year-old sister, Naomi (a pseudonym) following her everywhere and imitating her every move. They played dress-up (Naomi looked adorable in Terri's *Little House on the Prairie* sunbonnet), grocery shopping (their mom let them use real cans and boxes from the pantry), office assistant (Terri's hairbrush made an excellent telephone), and of course, school. Naomi willingly played any role Terri assigned to her in her funny, happy two-year-old way.

When Terri was eleven years old, she began babysitting neighborhood children. Her favorite activity was reading aloud to them. She would imitate her fifth grade teacher and practice different voices for all of the characters in the funny picture books the children loved. Terri taught her protégés how to sort shapes, make homemade Play-Doh, solve puzzles, and play Mousetrap, Lite-Brite, Pick-Up Sticks, and Hi-Ho! Cherry-O.

In college, Terri enrolled in early childhood development and completed a field experience with Head Start, a program for preschool children with disadvantaged backgrounds. She fell in love with those charming three- and four-year-old little people, who to her seemed like caricatures of adults. The children seemed to study their adults' every move and imitated their speech, mannerisms, facial expressions, and even dress.

Through these experiences, and later through her graduate coursework and the language that it offered her to describe them, Terri has come to see teaching as a way of being in the social world. It is like breathing. It is sometimes conscious and explicit, but it is always an awareness of how people learn from each other through observing, listening, and imitating actions, including language and how we speak. Terri asserts that she has been in the process of becoming a teacher since childhood through what Gee (1996) calls "mushfake" and which he defines as the process of trying on unfamiliar ways of speaking, being, and doing. Gee borrowed the term "mushfake" (Mack, 1989) from prison culture; it refers to making do with something less when the real thing is not available.

After her experience with Head Start, Terri took a job as a nanny, married a partner who was enlisted in the US Army, and continued her college career through various moves and duty stations. She was finally able to transfer enough courses to one institution to constitute a major. Upon earning her BA in English from the University of Maryland, European Division, she accepted a position as a substitute in secondary English teacher at the American School in Berlin, Germany.

Again, Terri quickly fell in love with the quirkiness of her students, now adolescents, who seemed to her like caricatures of their three-year-old selves—people who craved independence and who were serious observers of the world and all that they could learn from it. She realized how much she missed the familiar structures of the school day—bells, desks, and chalkboards.

Terri decided to pursue a teaching degree in secondary English education so that she could officially be licensed. She taught high school students in Georgia, Kentucky, and Puerto Rico. When her partner retired from the military, she returned to graduate school and has been a teacher educator ever since.

Out and Back Again

Terri remembers meeting Lauren during her first semester teaching secondary English methods in her current position. Terri was excited, and of course, nervous, to begin a new chapter in her teaching life. As a small, undergraduate, residential liberal arts college, this school was different from any other place she had taught. Although she had grown up in the area, she had been away for thirty years, following her partner's career and her own. She felt like an insider and an outsider simultaneously in the local community and at the college.

Terri credits Lauren for helping to facilitate these personal and professional transitions. Terri was in a new job at a new college, but she felt like an insider to the community because her parents and siblings still lived there. At the same time, she felt like an outsider. In her time away, she had gained experiences and an education that shifted her worldview. Like the authors of *This Fine Place So Far from Home: Voices of Academics from the Working Class* (Dews & Law, 1995), she was reconciling homecoming with her new identity as a professor of education committed to helping novice teachers develop social justice pedagogies.

Lauren was inquisitive, thoughtful, and eager to discuss the social justice ideals introduced in the secondary English methods course. Lauren told Terri about her involvement with Hands Across the World, a local organization supporting refugee families. Terri learned that in the years since her absence, Middletown (a pseudonym) had become a site for refugee resettlement. New families, many from Somalia, had been relocated there. Through Lauren and her involvement with the refugee relief organization, Terri was introduced to new communities and opportunities in Middletown.

Terri, however, realized that she had returned to a city marked by cultural, racial, linguistic, and religious tensions. Through Lauren's advocacy and active engagement with the Somali refugee community, Terri witnessed an alternative response to the historical and present realities of these social and political tensions in Middletown. As an "activist ally" (Swalwell, 2013), Lauren sought to model change in the narrative that parts of surrounding communities propelled. For example, she and a Somali student coauthored an article in a local newspaper to share the student's experience as a newcomer to the United States and to Middletown. Lauren also narrated counterstories about particular events that happened at her school in her first few years as a teacher (Rodriguez et al., 2017; Rodriguez et al., 2018). Through Lauren, Terri learned that caring teachers who are committed to social justice principles and practices can seamlessly cross the invisible borders that delineate communities.

Investment as Resistance

Terri sees herself as both an invested stayer and an invested leaver (Glazer, 2018). She exited secondary classroom teaching as an act of resistance to policies and practices that she felt were forced upon her and with which she disagreed. As a secondary classroom teacher, Terri felt the irony of being told to teach critical thinking skills while also telling students to "sit down and be quiet" for most of the day.

One day, after a brief absence, Terri returned to her classroom to find thirty desks in neat rows facing the chalkboard in the front of the room. That was not the way she had left it. Her ninth graders were in the middle of reading *Romeo and Juliet* in cooperative groups organized as acting companies. Desks were arranged in circles, or often pushed to the side when the scenes being been enacted required movement.

Upon her return, she was told that the school principal had ordered the desks moved to rows and silent reading. Although she quietly rearranged the desks and nothing was ever said about it, she couldn't help but feel the indictment—that somehow active learning was supposed to be something that occurred invisibly, silently, and individually in each student's head rather than visibly, audibly, and in interaction with others.

At the time, Terri didn't know that her teaching was constructivist or that constructivism is a legitimate and effective method. She only knew that the principal wanted silence and heads bowed over textbooks as he strode through the halls during classes. She now aims to help novice teachers develop the language and skills to defend their teaching choices. She urges her students to metaphorically break down the solid brick walls of schooling, especially in supporting vulnerable adolescents who are, as they should be, critically questioning the world around them.

In describing her experiences as a secondary English teacher to others, Terri considers what she felt to be her many roles: counselor, social worker, police officer, truant officer, language police, clothing monitor, and overall enforcer of rules for young people who are developmentally on target in their quest to challenge and resist the very rules and authority she felt pressured to enforce upon them.

For Terri, naming herself an invested stayer has multiple layers of meaning. As noted in the introduction, it is a form of resistance and a "refusal to do the job in certain ways or under certain conditions" (Glazer, 2018, p. 63). As in Glazer's study of teachers who exit, Terri's move was not just about securing a new career because she was not successful in the public school classroom. Instead it was conceptualized as an act of resistance to education policies and practices that were not aligned with her own.

Terri left secondary classroom teaching to resist, but she thinks of herself as a stayer rather than a leaver. She hopes to take up the concept of resistance through this new perspective.

This move in her professional identity (from *leaver* to *stayer*) is important because Terri has always felt like a quitter. Terri and her partner joke that she has quit more jobs than he will ever start because of their agreement that she would follow him in his military career. In her eight years as a licensed secondary teacher, she taught in five different schools in four different states.

When it was time for her partner to retire, Terri pursued graduate school. At the time, she was unfamiliar with the professional opportunities that would become available to her as a teacher educator. She resisted the idea that she was quitting teaching (or leaving the classroom as some of her colleagues termed it) and hoped to return to middle and secondary teaching when she finished her doctoral degree. Her graduate advisor, however, pointed out that as a college professor and teacher educator, she was still very much a teacher.

Although she misses many things about public school teaching, Terri does not miss its challenges and the ways she often felt forced to uphold practices and policies with which she disagreed. She still often feels like an imposter as she encourages novice teachers to embrace challenges and to resist practices and policies with which they disagree. She realizes this is much more easily said than done, especially given the physical, intellectual, and political freedoms that she now enjoys as a college professor. She continually asks herself, "How can I leverage these particular circumstances within this particular context as an act of resistance and agency?"

LEANING INTO THE WORK

Lauren and Terri share a unique vision of hope for their work as social justice educators. They lean into their work in response to challenges and together consider how they will draw from their own strengths and the strengths of their students in order to thrive. When Lauren started her career, someone told her that the worst part of teaching would be "The Three P's"—parents, politics, and paperwork. She didn't know it then, but she feels now that the politics part of the adage is sometimes too true. Lauren and Terri are both more and more aware of how politics—and not just educational politics—affect the learning climate of classrooms and the social climate of their work.

Lauren and Terri hope to educate citizens so that they can astutely navigate sometimes rocky circumstances and advocate for themselves and their communities to make positive change. Lauren's students are empathetic, proud, and inventive. They are multilingual learners who are starting to learn English as young adults. Many are refugees; some are voluntary immigrants. A large number of her students were born in refugee camps in East Africa. It is a long jump (physically and figuratively) from that life to one in the midwestern United States.

Even so, Lauren and Terri believe these students arrive to a community that, at least in certain spaces, is a welcoming place to land. The public school they attend does have some Somali teachers and a Somali principal, which isn't everything, but it's certainly part of welcoming. Lauren and Terri envision the community becoming more secure in its tone of welcoming.

In their experiences in Middletown, Lauren and Terri agree that some people are good at holding on to old traditions and perhaps not so good at being flexible with the new. Lauren sees this, too, in some of her school's spaces. Often, the students are more responsive to each other than to the teachers. Another part of welcoming is continuing to welcome. One cannot meet students at the classroom door and welcome them in—"Hola! Sidee tahay?"—only to expect them to conform to every traditional school norm, whether it suits them or not.

Through their extended professional relationship, Lauren and Terri have continued conversations about how to better support EL students with refugee and immigrant backgrounds. They conduct pedagogical research and present at professional conferences together. Researching and writing about the experiences of traditionally marginalized people in their community sustains them and helps them to thrive as social justice–oriented educators with a shared investment in the future.

REFERENCES

Dews, C., and Law, C. (Eds). (1995). *This fine place so far from home: Voices of academics from the working class.* Philadelphia: Temple University Press.

Gee, J. P. (1996). *Social linguistics and literacies: Ideology in discourses* (2nd ed.). Philadelphia, PA: Falmer Press.

Glazer, J. (2018). Learning from those who no longer teach: Viewing teacher attrition through a resistance lens. *Teaching and Teacher Education, 74*, 62-71.

Gorski, P. C. (2014). *Reaching and teaching students in poverty: Strategies for erasing the opportunity gap.* New York, NY: Teachers College Press.

Gorski, P. C., & Swalwell, K. (2015). Equity literacy for all. *Educational Leadership , 72*(6), 34-40.

Grant, C. A., & Sleeter, C. E. (2006). *Turning on learning: Five approaches for multicultural teaching plans for race, class, gender and disability* (4th ed.). San Francisco: Jossey-Bass.

Holland, D., Lachicotte, W., Jr., Skinner, D., & Cain, C. (1998). *Identity and agency in cultural worlds.* Cambridge, MA: Harvard University Press.

Ladson-Billings, G. (2005). Reading, writing, and race: Literacy practices of teachers in diverse classrooms. In T. L. McCarty (Ed.), *Language, literacy, and power in schooling* (pp. 133-150). London: Lawrence Erlbaum.

Ladson-Billings, G. (2006). Yes, but how do we do it?: Practicing culturally relevant pedagogy. In J. Landsman & C. W. Lewis (Eds.), *White teachers, diverse classrooms: A guide to building inclusive schools, promoting high expectations, and eliminating racism.* (pp. 30-42). Sterling, VA: Stylus.

Mack, N. (1989). The social nature of words: Voices, dialogues, quarrels. *The Writing Instructor, 8*, 157-165.

Rodriguez, T. L., & Cho, H. (2011). Eliciting critical literacy narratives of bi/multilingual teacher candidates across U.S. teacher education contexts. *Teaching and Teacher Education, 27*(3), 496-504.

Rodriguez, T. L., Bohn-Gettler, C. M., Israelson, M. H., O'Brien, M. A., & Thoma, L. B. (2017). Telling our stories: Navigating social justice-oriented teaching on the ground. In H. Hallman (Ed.), *Innovations in English language arts teacher education.* Castle Hill: Emerald Press.

Rodriguez, T. L., Mahalingappa, L., Evangeliste, M., & Thoma, L. (2018). Educators must be activists: Advocating for Muslim students. *The European Educational Researcher, 1*(2), 117-135. doi: 10.31757/euer.123

Santoro, D. A. (2018). *Demoralized: Why teachers leave the profession they love and how they can stay.* Cambridge, MA: Harvard Education Press.

Swalwell, K. (2013). *Educating activist allies: Social justice pedagogy with the suburban and urban elite.* New York, NY: Routledge.

Chapter Two

Reciprocity for Critically Conscious Teacher Education

Allison J. Spenader and Leah Shepard-Carey

This chapter explores the reciprocal nature of the professional development of two teacher educators. The narrative follows our evolution as English as a second language (ESL) teachers as our praxis takes on new and expanding areas of focus. Our ongoing relationship is described through the presentation of vignettes that illustrate key moments when we engage in meaningful explorations of critical approaches to teacher education. With the changing field of ESL education, preservice teachers are expected to provide standards-based instruction, but also to be advocates for our emergent bilingual students.

We employ the term *emergent bilingual*s from García and Kleifgen (2018) to recognize the rich and diverse linguistic repertoires of English language learners (ELLs) who continue to be marginalized in public schooling (García & Flores, 2014). While the terms English learner and emergent bilingual are not synonymous, the latter more accurately reflects a more critical perspective on the field of ESL and better recognizes the multilingual capabilities of ELLs. With increasing calls for teachers to develop critical consciousness (Kubanyiova & Crookes, 2016; Motha, 2014) and engage in culturally and linguistically sustaining approaches (Paris & Alim, 2014), teacher educators become responsible for developing programs and courses that align with these calls.

While teacher educators typically engage in research and professional development, we suggest that mentoring and collegial relationships have the power to influence transformative change in practice and teacher development. Drawing on literature in ESL education, critical approaches to education, and notions of professional development and mentorship, we share vignettes that illustrate key moments when we engaged in meaningful explorations of critical approaches to teacher education.

Through reflection of reciprocal professional relationships in teacher education, the field can begin to interrogate the necessity of colleagues who push our practices and thinking across time and space. Specifically, for English language teaching and learning, this reciprocity is integral to developing critically conscious language educators who consider how race, language, and power intersect in everyday teaching.

ENGLISH AS A SECOND LANGUAGE: TOWARD CRITICALITY IN THE FIELD

In what follows, we share a brief overview of the roots and movements toward more critical approaches in ESL education in the United States, which provides the context for our narrative. ESL education has undergone significant changes since *Lau v. Nichols* (Douglas & Supreme Court of the United States, 1973), the legislation that mandated that students with developing English proficiency receive supplemental support in English. With more than 4.5 million students identified as English learners in the United States (National Center for Educational Statistics, 2017), and many more who are multilingual, structural and philosophical shifts in programming are a necessity.

Structurally, ESL program delivery can take many forms, and generally requires teachers to be able to support students at any proficiency level and in any content area. The fact that the teachers are expected to meet such diverse needs is in itself challenging. Further complicating the picture are national and state shifts in curriculum and assessments, as well as new guidelines ushered in as part of the Every Student Succeeds Act (2015).

Additionally, program models for delivering ESL instruction vary widely between states and even within states. Teachers are not only asked to meet the needs of their learners but are also expected to constantly adapt their instruction to meet different program needs, for example when a district moves from a pull-out model to a co-teaching model. In light of changes in the field and with the advent of new College and Career Readiness Standards developed as part of the Common Core State Standards (2010), teachers' purview is shifting to include increased focus on providing leadership and advocacy within schools (TESOL International Association, 2016).

While the United States does not have an official language, implicit and explicit English-only policies in schools and communities reinforce negative perceptions of multilingualism and affect teachers' practices (Motha, 2014). For example, the vast majority of emergent bilinguals in the United States are currently educated in English-dominant contexts (García & Kleifgen, 2018), which means that students do not have access to instruction in their home language. Efforts in curriculum and standards design have also emphasized the importance of emergent bilinguals' access to academic language to close what has been called the "achievement gap," which of course is a well-intentioned effort. Yet emergent bilinguals may miss out on enriching opportunities to expand their linguistic repertoires and engage in deeper thinking opportunities because of perceived needs for remediation and gaps in academic language (Adair et al., 2017).

Flores and Rosa (2015) explicate the racialized nature of deficit views, and even question additive approaches to language learning in schools because it spreads a discourse of "linguistic appropriateness" (how to use language and for what purposes) that is grounded in the white gaze. Toni Morrison describes *white gaze* as privileging whiteness as the norm and positioning others who deviate from white standards and practices as deficit. Such biases have historically positioned people of color and nonnative speakers as inferior. Motha (2014) similarly explains the influence of colonialism and globalization on English-language speakers, which has perpetuated notions of native-speaker proficiency, accent bias, and the overall hegemony of a "standard" English language at the cost of local languages and dialects.

Culturally and linguistically sustaining pedagogies and multilingual approaches hold the power to resist monoglossic norms and integrate students' identities in the curriculum. Kubanyiova and Crookes (2016) recognize language teachers as "moral agents" of change, who should be trained to implement critically conscious practices. We join in making recommendations for building critical consciousness about language practices and ideologies in language teacher preparation programs and suggestions for multilingual pedagogies (e.g., Goodwin & Jiménez, 2015; Motha, 2014).

Educators also require spaces and dialogic opportunities to trouble and reflect on their own practice. One avenue, as evidenced in the narratives that follow, is mentoring. Mentoring can be formal or informal, yet it is pivotal in the development of critically oriented language teachers and programs.

PROFESSIONAL DEVELOPMENT AND MENTORSHIP

What inspires innovations necessary to advance critical pedagogies? ESL preservice teachers receive information and skills training as part of a structured program designed to provide them with what they need to work effectively in schools. Postgraduation, teachers further hone their practice through real-world teaching experiences. The cycle frequently continues with graduate-level studies and ongoing professional development provided by professional organizations and school districts.

So much of the foundational understandings of what ESL teaching embodies, and how it should operate, stems from those initial years in a preservice teacher education program. The experience preservice teachers receive as part of their initial licensure training lays the groundwork for how a teacher's praxis will develop. Hence, ESL teacher preparation must be responsive to the needs of schools and those of emergent bilinguals. Faculty members working within such programs bear a responsibility to partake in ongoing and critical reflection on their work as teacher educators.

Professional development through conferences and ongoing attention to current research helps faculty members maintain their understanding of trends. In teacher education, there is a perpetual cycle of learning informed by work with colleagues, students, and cooperating teachers in the field. Each of these sources contributes to a teacher educator's work in unique and valuable ways. One particularly interesting source of professional development is the mentorship relationship that develops between faculty members and graduates from their programs.

At a recent welcome-back-to-campus meeting, Hinton (2019), the president of a small liberal arts college, shared her own experiences around mentorship. As a first-generation undergraduate, she had received the following invitation from a caring faculty mentor: *Will you allow me to journey with you?* When Allison heard this story, she immediately thought of her own journey with Leah, her coauthor and former student. There are powerful implications embedded in a request such as the one Hinton described. Embarking on a mutually sustaining relationship of professional development would result in not only deeper conversations around equity and advocacy within the field of ESL but also the reframing of a program.

Research on mentorship explores the relationships between mentors and protégés; the potential benefits of mentorship for the mentee are numerous and have been widely described (e.g., Baldwin et al., 2008; Turner, 2015). The functions of mentorship can be broadly conceptualized as falling into two categories: academic or career functions and psychosocial functions. Mentoring relationships move through cycles: initiation, cultivation, separation, and eventually collegiality (Kram, 1988). There are tangible benefits to the mentor as well. Johnson and Ridley (2018) describe how many faculty members enjoy intrinsic benefits of mentorship, including a sense of rejuvenation and the excitement and satisfaction of working with and supporting an enthusiastic colleague in the field. Our relationship has followed the mentoring cycle outlined above and has been mutually beneficial for both of our professional trajectories.

The mentoring relationship evolved and shifted as Leah's roles change, and as her work oscillates between a research-intensive graduate program and her alma mater. This retrospective analysis explores how reciprocity within mentorship can provide the impetus for ongoing professional development, leading to increasingly critically conscious language education within the field of teacher education. Beginning with the origins of an ESL licensure program at a small midwestern liberal-arts college, our story considers how trends in the field of ESL teaching have shifted over time, necessitating ongoing reflection and reconsideration of how to prepare critically oriented teachers.

THE LAUNCH OF A NEW ESL LICENSURE PROGRAM

When the college where Allison currently teaches sought to develop a new K–12 ESL licensure program, she was hired in part due to her experiences as an ESL and English as a foreign language (EFL) teacher and her Master of Arts in Teaching English as a Second Language (MATESL) degree. The institution felt strongly that there was a growing need in the region for ESL teachers and was supportive of Allison during her first years as a novice faculty member embarking on creating a new licensure program. Through collaboration with colleagues from her graduate school and contacts at numerous institutions, she developed a program of study that was approved by the state in 2011.

The design of the licensure program was not unlike those of peer institutions. It included courses on pedagogical grammar, linguistics and second language acquisition, and second language literacy and assessment, as well as an ESL pedagogy course and a theoretical foundations course. A focus on communicative language teaching within traditional pull-out and sheltered models of instruction reflected current practices in the field since the 1990s. The pull-out model was prevalent and based on the idea that the emergent bilinguals were best served by targeted language instruction. Following the development of some predetermined level of acceptable proficiency, they would be allowed to join the mainstream classroom. ESL teachers were primarily responsible for language proficiency development, and as students advanced, academic language related to the content areas was woven into the instruction. Yet this model was about to change, reflecting significant shifts in thinking about how ESL instruction should be delivered and what role the ESL teacher should play.

Allison's training in ESL had focused on building a thorough understanding of the mechanics of *Standard North American English* and an embedded understanding that this variety would serve as the goal of all ESL (and even EFL) instruction. Conversations around the racism implied in a term such as *Standard English* would not emerge for another decade. Debates around the problematic nature of the term *native speaker* were only a few years off (Motha, 2014). While she had wondered about dilemmas around the political power of English, and the prevalence of *white savior* viewpoints (Cammarota, 2011) sometimes expressed among ESL teachers and teacher candidates, these topics received relatively little formal attention in her preparation.

A lone course on sociolinguistics provided a foundational overview of the privilege and power associated with the English language. At the time, ESL teachers were expected to provide support for learners of English, designing lessons focused on the development of language proficiency. Cultural content was encouraged and often presented from the viewpoint of the teacher, who most frequently represented a white, middle-class cis-gender female perspective.

Furthermore, the very pedagogies employed by ESL teachers largely reflected a Euro-American perspective on teaching and learning, often lacking attention to issues of inequities within the schools and classrooms where they occurred. As Liggett (2007) describes, white ESL teachers run the risk of "disadvantaging the very students they seek to empower by not knowing the ways in which their racial and cultural membership informs the decisions they make about teaching" (p. 46).

The relative lack of attention paid to issues of critical consciousness within the field of ESL at the time was on the verge of changing. While the seeds of understanding the important role culturally and linguistically sustaining practices had been planted in her ESL training program, through practice in the field, discussions and self-reflection, and significant movement within the profession, Allison's commitment to more critical approaches grew.

While the first candidates to come through the program were few, their enthusiasm for teaching ESL and working with language learners brought passion and energy to the program. Allison and her first cohort of students experienced a particularly strong bond; they felt a sense of solidarity in embarking on something new and important. Among this first cohort was an enthusiastic preservice teacher seeking both Spanish and ESL licensure: Leah.

Working Lunches

Within the first years of the new program's existence, significant shifts in scope and focus necessitated a rethinking of course content. Of critical importance to this work was feedback from recent graduates. Leah was first hired in an elementary school located close to her college, where she taught for nearly two years before beginning her graduate studies at the same institution where Allison had completed her doctorate. We began a tradition of back-to-school lunches, checking in before the start of each new school year.

Leah's new status as a graduate student ushered her into the role of teacher educator. Leah sought to gain insights about teaching and mentoring preservice teachers, as well as navigating her graduate school experience.

Leah found herself now a colleague of Allison's friends and former classmates, and social and professional circles were overlapping and converging. The lunches also provided valuable new insights to Allison. Leah was able to share her evolving perspectives on her own teacher preparation in light of her graduate-level coursework and conversations with professionals from another institution.

Allison's thinking about the ESL licensure program was influenced further by a series of presentations that she and Leah listened to and later discussed over lunch at local and regional conferences. Keynote addresses would frequently cause us to linger in hallways and over coffee at the lunch table, considering how the work of researchers in the field would influence the courses we were teaching. These meetings provided dynamic opportunities for both of us to think through the merits of new perspectives and challenges of ESL instruction.

Return to the Alma Mater

Allison's early support and advising during Leah's undergraduate years became the roots for Leah's sustained interest in more equitable English language education. With a few years of teaching and Allison's encouragement and connections, Leah began graduate school with the aim of becoming a teacher educator. During these first few years in graduate school, Leah was immersed in the changing field of language education and became committed to developing more critical consciousness and equitable practices in her own teacher education courses.

As the conversations between us shifted from discussing Leah's public school teaching to her new role as a teacher educator, there was a sense of camaraderie as we shared our ideas and dilemmas. When it was time for Allison to make arrangements for sabbatical, she asked Leah if she would be interested in teaching her course, Theoretical Foundations of ESL Teaching. Leah was thrilled at the prospect of teaching the course and returning to her alma mater.

As Leah prepared for the course, this journey offered new opportunities to integrate research that questioned the state of English language education and promoted more critically oriented practices in schools. These additions to the course included new texts, such as Motha's (2014) *Race, Empire, and English Language Teaching* and dialogic opportunities for students to reflect on their own language practices and ideologies. Early in her graduate school career, Leah had read Motha's (2014) text, which profoundly changed her thinking and practice on ESL teaching; thus she thought it might prove to be meaningful for students in the course.

Leah and another graduate school colleague planned a discussion of the text between their undergraduate preservice teachers because they thought that some sort of exchange might produce rich discussions, inclusive of a variety of perspectives and experiences. They created a structured discussion activity (Gopalakrishnan & Shepard-Carey, forthcoming). They intentionally paired students, provided a guide for discussion, and then had the students arrange their own discussions via an online platform. Post-discussion, each student turned in a reflection that discussed not only their insights from the book, but also the discussion itself. Corresponding reflections and discussions demonstrated that the activity was highly engaging and meaningful to students. Furthermore, after the activity, the students in the course at Allison's institution elucidated their increased awareness of linguistic and racial bias and specific action steps they would take as future teachers to engage in more culturally and linguistically sustaining practice.

With the addition of new critically oriented texts and activities, students also left the course with a better understanding of how power structures shape languages and our teaching. With Allison's encouragement to modify the syllabus and activities, Leah was able to work toward developing future educators who would think more critically about their own practice. Allison's support of these changes signified a mutual trust and commitment to improving teacher education and further reflected the enduring collegiality that we had built.

Sabbatical: Notes from the Home Office

While Leah's journey toward a career as a preservice teacher educator was undergoing additional changes due to her experiences back at her alma mater, Allison found time and space to focus on course design and scholarship during her sabbatical. While Allison successfully gained tenure at her institution, she continued to feel the pressure to improve the quality of the ESL licensure program in light of changing demands on teachers in her field.

The midcareer years of a faculty member are often seen as a time for professional reflection and reassessment of teaching and scholarship, but these years can also be marred by increased expectations and workload obligations to the institutions. Baldwin and colleagues (2008) recommend that midcareer faculty utilize networking and collaboration as a means of refreshing their teaching praxis, and collaboration with Leah became an important source of new thinking around the needs of the program.

While not on campus, she was able to follow Leah's approach to the ESL theory course through the online course management system. She watched as Leah introduced the new text and designed challenging and provocative discussion questions. She could see how the level of discourse she was expecting from these undergraduate students was demanding more critically conscious thinking about issues of race and identity. Leah was pushing her students to examine their privilege in new ways and to see themselves as advocates for their learners within schools and communities. It was truly exciting to see how Leah's approach to this one course would have implications on other courses in the sequence, including courses on literacy, assessment, pedagogy, and even pedagogical grammar.

The semester-long sabbatical also provided time for focus on new and ongoing research endeavors. Allison's research on content-based instruction in foreign language contexts took a cue from her new thinking around critical approaches to language teaching. A new study was undertaken, looking specifically at how foreign language teachers incorporated themes of critical and social justice in their instruction. This new study pushed the envelope in foreign language teaching in two ways: it implores foreign language teachers to teach in a content-driven approach (an approach common in ESL), and it also encourages these classrooms to embed meaningful content that deals with social justice issues. The momentum for such a study had been building over the years and was influenced significantly by conversations with co-investigators and respected colleagues, including Leah.

At the end of the sabbatical and Leah's teaching of the theoretical foundations course, we met again for a working lunch. Both of us felt excitement around the direction in which our journeys as teacher educators were headed. One outcome of effective mentorship is finding one's voice (Griffin et al., 2015). Mentees report that through the relationships that developed, they could both identify their professional goals/purposes and exert more agency.

For us, this effect was mutual; both of us benefit from the reciprocal nature of the mentorship. Leah was encouraged by the positive feedback she received from her students and the depth of critical thinking she was able to elicit from these preservice teachers. Leah's teaching reinvigorated Allison's conceptualization of other courses in the sequence. Allison has developed more courage to take an increasingly critical stance within her courses, and she felt encouraged by the data Leah had gathered as part of the discussions she facilitated between the preservice teachers at the two different institutions.

The theoretical foundations course underwent a complete redesign, shifting primary focus away from traditional understandings of second language acquisition processes and sociocultural issues influencing the experiences of ESL students and teachers. Instead, the course became a time and place for critical discourse around multilingual and multicultural identities, ethical dilemmas regarding teaching and systems of schooling, and exploring teachers' roles in advocacy for ESL students, their families, and their teachers. Instrumental to this shift in focus were Leah's additions to course readings and discussion prompts, and ongoing conversations between us around the evolving role of the ESL educator.

RECIPROCITY AND COLLEGIALITY

The reciprocal benefits of our ongoing mentorship is clear. Our scholarship and teaching have been influenced by conversations and feedback we receive from each other in a myriad of social and professional contexts. Professionally, both of us recognize the need for ESL teacher education to focus on culturally and linguistically sustaining practices, and we are committed to crafting coursework to meet those ends. Motha (2014) urges ESL teacher education to focus on the development of teachers by employing a "focus on teacher agency, applying a specific and deliberate emphasis on the role that teachers play in shaping the power relations, access to resources, and positionality of our linguistic minority students" (p. 141).

Mentorship has allowed for a sharing of ideas and resources for educating preservice teachers to recognize how their own linguistic, racial, and cultural identities shape their perspectives as ESL teachers. We commit to challenging our students to develop their agency for critically conscious language teaching. As the field of ESL teaching increasingly recognizes the harmful effects of monolingual and colonial perspectives on English instruction, this new generation of teachers will be positioned to take on leadership roles in their schools and communities.

Our work together is not finished. The mentoring relationship continues as the mentor-mentee roles undergo shapeshifting, and the directionality of the relationship becomes more fluid. Moreover, like the preservice teachers in our programs, we know that we must continue to work toward being "moral agents" of change (Kubanyiova & Crookes, 2016) who engage in critically conscious teacher education practice, which further requires ongoing research and professional development.

Mentoring and collegial relationships remain integral to our growth. As Leah realizes her goals in research and teaching, she will assume the role of faculty mentor for her students. We will continue to work within the mentoring stage that Kram (1988) calls *collegiality*. Hinton's (2019) powerful message, *Will you allow me to journey with you?* encapsulates our ongoing relationship as women poised to support and challenge each other in an effort to provide more equitable education for emergent bilingual students.

REFERENCES

Adair, J. K., Colegrove, K. S. S., & McManus, M. E. (2017). How the word gap argument negatively impacts young children of Latinx immigrants' conceptualizations of learning. *Harvard Educational Review, 87*(3), 309–334.

Baldwin, R., DeZure, D., Shaw, A., & Moretto, K. (2008). Mapping the terrain of mid-career faculty at a research university: Implications for faculty and academic leaders. *Change: The Magazine of Higher Learning, 40*(5), 46–55.

Cammarota, J. (2011). Blindsided by the avatar: White saviors and allies out of Hollywood and in education. *Review of Education, Pedagogy, and Cultural Studies, 33*(3), 242–259.

Common Core State Standards. (2010). National Governors Association Center for Best Practices and Council of Chief State School Officers, Washington, DC.

Douglas, W. O., & Supreme Court of the United States. (1973). U.S. Reports: Lau v. Nichols, 414 U.S. 563.

Every Student Succeeds Act. (2015). Retrieved November 5, 2019 from https://www.congress.gov/bill/114th-congress/senate-bill/1177

Flores, N., & Rosa, J. (2015). Undoing appropriateness: Raciolinguistic ideologies and language diversity in education. *Harvard Educational Review, 85*(2), 149–171.

García, O., & Flores, N. (2014). Multilingualism and common core state standards in the United States. In S. May (Ed.), *The multilingual turn: Implications for SLA, TESOL, and bilingual education.* London, UK: Routledge.

García, O., & Kleifgen, J. A. (2018). *Educating emergent bilinguals: Policies, programs, and practices for English learners.* New York, NY: Teachers College Press.

Goodwin, A. P., & Jiménez, R. (2015). TRANSLATE: New strategic approaches for English learners. *The Reading Teacher, 69*(6), 621–625.

Gopalakrishnan, A., & Shepard-Carey, L. (forthcoming). Developing critical language awareness in future language teachers: Engaging in inter-college conversations. In M. Jeon, M. Figueredo, & F. Carra-Salsberg (Eds.), *Globally informed design and praxis in languages, literatures and linguistics curricula.*

Griffin, K., Eury, J., & Gaffney, M. (2015). Digging deeper: Exploring the relationship between mentoring, developmental interactions, and student agency. *New Directions for Higher Education, 2015*(171), 13–22. doi:10.1002/he.20138

Hinton, M. D. (2019, August). Welcome. *Faculty/Academic Affairs Workshop.* Talk presented at the Faculty/Academic Affairs Workshop, College of St. Benedict and St. John's University, St. Joseph, MN, USA.

Johnson, W., & Ridley, C. (2018). *The elements of mentoring* (2nd ed.). New York, NY: Palgrave Macmillan.

Kram, K. (1988). *Mentoring at work: Developmental relationships in organizational life.* Lanham, MD: University Press of America.

Kubanyiova, M., & Crookes, G. (2016). Re-envisioning the roles, tasks, and contributions of language teachers in the multilingual era of language education research and practice. *The Modern Language Journal, 100*(S1), 117–132.

Liggett, T. (2007). The alchemy of identity: The role of white racial identity in the teaching and pedagogy of new ESOL teachers. In M. Mantero (Ed.), *Identity and second language learning.* Charlotte, NC: Information Age Publishing.

National Center for Educational Statistics: English language learners in public schools. (2017). Retrieved from https://nces.ed.gov/programs/coe/indicator_cgf.asp#info

Motha, S. (2014). *Race, empire, and English language teaching: Creating responsible and ethical anti-racist practice.* New York, NY: Teachers College Press.

Paris, D., & Alim, H. S. (2014). What are we seeking to sustain through culturally sustaining pedagogy? A loving critique forward. *Harvard Educational Review, 84*(1), 85–100.

TESOL International Association. (2016). *The preparation of the ESL educator in the era of college- and career-readiness standards.* Alexandria, VA: Author.

Turner, C. S. (Ed.). (2015). *Mentoring as transformative practice: Supporting student and faculty diversity.* Retrieved from https://ebookcentral.proquest.com

Chapter Three

Lessons for Special Education Teachers to Persist and Thrive

Shelley Neilsen Gatti, Martin Odima Jr., Deeqaifrah Hussein, and L. Lynn Stansberry Brusnahan

This chapter highlights faculty (Shelley and Lynn) and graduate student authors (Martin and Deeqaifrah) as special educators who share the goal of working for equity and inclusive practices from diverse racial and ethnic identities and professional experiences. As invested stayers in education, they offer recommendations to help other special educators persist and thrive. It begins with a discussion of the challenges related to retaining special education teachers of color. We then share how commitments to racial and social justice motivate us to persist. The chapter highlights how our connections enhance professional growth, build social capital, and provide collegial support that sustains us and helps us to thrive.

SPECIAL EDUCATION TEACHER DIVERSITY AND RETENTION

Special education teachers evaluate, plan, intervene, monitor, and use technology to support students learning while collaborating with families, general education teachers, and specialists. The workload for all educators is intense, and for special educators it may be even greater (Stempien & Loeb, 2002). Special education teachers respond to a wide range of instructional needs, navigate the nuances of multiple classrooms, and manage large caseloads. These demands often lead to challenges with recruitment and retention.

For decades, there have been concerns about special education teacher supply and attrition (Boe & Cook, 2006). Despite efforts to address these issues, the US Department of Education (2015-2016) reports a critical shortage of special education personnel. This shortage is compounded by teachers leaving the profession within their first few years. Nationally, more than 30 percent of new teachers leave during their first three years of teaching and more than 50 percent leave within the next five years (Educators 4 Excellence, 2015). Special education teachers leave the profession at nearly double the rate of general education teachers (National Coalition on Personnel Shortages in Special Education, 2014).

Teacher retention is important in all license areas, but it is especially critical for teachers of color. Teacher of color turnover has been found to be 18–24 percent higher than white teacher turnover (Ingersoll & May, 2011). This is problematic because a nondiverse teaching corps is a consistent barrier to producing strong racially equitable education outcomes (Sanchez, 2015). Villegas and Irvine (2010) report that students of color accrue academic benefits when taught by a same-race teacher or when exposed to a teaching force (at the school or district level) that is racially/ethnically representative of the student population.

LESSONS LEARNED

Shelley and Lynn, who both identify as white special education teacher educators, are inspired by Martin's and Deeqaifrah's journeys because they understand the critical importance of supporting special education teachers of color. They share Martin's and Deeqaifrah's stories (see the end of the chapter) in their courses and actively create spaces to prepare future educators for the realities of the profession. Here, we reflect upon how our experiences, collaborations, and relationships play a role in our collective persistence.

Lesson One: Sphere of Influence

Martin and Deeqaifrah seek opportunities to formally study specially designed education and to use innovative approaches to meet learning needs. They use their knowledge and work within their spheres of influence (Covey, 2004) to creatively solve problems and improve educational access for students. Martin, a special education paraprofessional seeking licensure, was accepted into a public/private partnership program between the university and the state to increase teacher diversity (Collaborative Urban Education Scholarship Program, n.d.). As a graduate student and teacher-in-training, he felt challenged by systems that restricted opportunity and segregated students of color with disabilities. He learned, for example, that students who are misidentified or denied access to appropriate services are at risk for unequal educational opportunities, underachievement, and dropping out of school (Gargiulo & Bouck, 2018).

When Martin discovered that his students didn't receive science instruction, he collaborated with others to provide science learning opportunities. He asked friends in a science doctoral program to brainstorm science activities appropriate for students with disabilities. He recruited college students to volunteer at the school and developed the Hope Science Program (HSP) with the goal of creating opportunities for both college and elementary students to actively engage in science, regardless of their ability. For the first time, the students in the special education program participated in the school's science fair, and Martin realized he could interrupt systems.

Martin also began utilizing Universal Design for Learning (UDL) principles to change the way he planned and implemented instruction. UDL is a framework that seeks to make learning accessible for all students (CAST, 2018). Martin uses UDL to promote choice in how students demonstrate competency and knowledge, design engaging lessons, and identify different ways to make material accessible to students. Through UDL, not only do students with disabilities benefit, but all students are able to learn together, which in turn fosters a more inclusive environment at the school overall. Lynn and Shelley have recruited Martin to teach university courses and share his examples of UDL implementation.

Deeqaifrah's sphere of influence comes through her roles as a parent and a general education teacher. She understands the power of individualized education program plans (IEPs) and how plans benefit students when they include clear and transparent educational goals. After moving into an itinerant position, Deeqaifrah supported other teachers in implementing IEPs, differentiating instruction, and incorporating evidence-based practices and behavioral supports for students. Lynn, who is also a parent of a child with special needs, mentored Deeqaifrah to move into roles where her influence would have an impact.

As a special education teacher, Deeqaifrah very quickly learned that significant cultural barriers to immigrant families' understanding of special education systems and services exist. She noticed that families in diverse communities continuously declined special education services due to social stigma and anxiety related to special education. Parents learned from other members of their community that once schools identified students with disabilities, they were often secluded from their general education peers and even sent to different schools. Sometimes this led to families withdrawing from special education or leaving the local district and enrolling their students in charter schools.

Through her connections with parent organizations, she set up proactive strategies for teaching families how to connect with their school team and navigate cultural barriers. At the beginning of each academic year, Deeqaifrah encourages families to connect with teachers and share their children's strengths and areas of concern. After consulting with university faculty and cultural liaisons, Deeqaifrah advocated for special education introductory seminars for families. She helps colleagues and community leaders discuss cultural barriers and investigate ways to support students and families while reducing barriers to education.

Lesson Two: Tough Conversations

Special education teachers already face challenging conversations with their colleagues, and special education teachers of color deal with such conversations for their students and for themselves. In their work studying the experiences of black male teachers, Bristol and Goings (2018) recommend that teacher preparation programs include strategies for navigating potentially racist school workplace environments. Martin and Deeqaifrah often spoke with Shelley and Lynn about how they engage in tough conversations with their white colleagues and witness fellow staff of color marginalized, disrespected, and dismissed while white teachers resist difficult conversations on race.

Further, the competency and preparation of teachers of color is often questioned (Bristol, 2015). Black male teachers report that they are rarely recognized for their pedagogy and content knowledge (Bryan & Ford, 2014; Jackson & Knight-Manuel, 2018). When Deeqaifrah started out as a special education teacher, she anticipated the typical challenges that many new special educators experience. What she didn't anticipate—and struggled with the most—were structural barriers and the critical questioning of others regarding her competency. Her colleagues didn't recognize her experience as a general education teacher, and they anticipated her struggling with students with challenging behavior.

When she reached out to these colleagues for support, she felt judged, even though she often worked overtime to complete paperwork. Having a supportive relationship with Shelley and Lynn was beneficial. She shared with them that she often received "back-handed compliments." For example, a white colleague once said, "You are so smart and so articulate." Sometimes Deeqaifrah smiled and moved on in response to these "compliments," lacking the energy to call out these uncomfortable comments. Other times her response led to an expression of white fragility. When white colleagues responded with "I don't see color," Deeqaifrah felt that if they didn't see color, they didn't see her.

Deeqaifrah noticed that white colleagues no longer spoke freely around her and stopped including her in social events. Sadly, this is not uncommon for teachers of color. According to Goings (2015), black male teachers encounter colleagues who will both covertly and overtly treat them as social outcasts. Deeqaifrah persists by remembering her personal and professional mission as a special education teacher, and she does everything she can to educate herself and obtain positions where she can interrupt systems and make progress for other teachers, students, and their families.

Martin's experiences are similar, although his school community keeps conversations about racial equity and access at the forefront. The school maintains a diverse student body in terms of race/ethnicity, economic/social class, and English-language abilities. Martin credits his elementary school's administration for allowing space to have discussions about race and its impact on staff and students of color in ways that foster, rather than limit, "the ability to form authentic connections across racial lines" (DiAngelo, 2011, p. 66). Without training, talking, time, and leadership, these kinds of racial hierarchies, racist interactions, and microaggressions would most likely occur more often at Martin's school.

Special education teachers will remain in the profession if there are strong avenues for communication and trust between general education teachers, special education teachers, support staff, and other related-service professionals (Bettini et al., 2018). Educators need avenues for these difficult conversations. Listening and learning from Deeqaifrah and Martin about their experiences led Shelley and Lynn to incorporate course content that more deeply explores the role of white privilege and bias. They now include strategies for candidates of color to navigate potentially challenging racist workplaces.

Lesson Three: Hone Teaching Skills to Increase Efficacy and Expertise

Martin and Deeqaifrah combat negative perceptions of their professionalism through advanced training. During his first years of teaching, Martin's district launched an ambitious technology initiative. Martin built expertise through a grant-funded graduate project focusing on evidence-based practices and technology to make education more equitable, inclusive, and accessible. When his district implemented a one-to-one program, Martin's classroom served as an experimental site. Martin's school acknowledged the large learning curve for teachers and found several ways to shift differentiated instruction and evidence-based strategies to the core of instruction and daily routines through professional development, teacher-to-teacher coaching, and establishing a flexible network for implementing technological ideas in the classroom. Martin was asked to coach other teachers and established himself as a teacher-leader. His efforts contributed to his elementary school being named an Apple Distinguished School, affecting the district's use of technology in the classroom.

Deeqaifrah developed her expertise formally, both by gaining additional special education teaching licenses and through relationships with university faculty. In her role as an itinerant teacher, colleagues looked to her to provide resources on evidence-based practices in the classrooms. She helped new special education teachers implement positive behavior intervention strategies and specific interventions for students with disabilities. Through her connections with the university, she earned a reputation as a resourceful colleague within her department. Furthermore, she has since earned her emotional behavioral disability license and special education director's license and is working on her doctorate in educational leadership. She will start this school year as one of the special education directors in her large urban district.

Lesson Four: Engage in Professional Collaborations

We agree that professional collaborations have enabled us to enhance our professional growth, contribute to the field, and access sustained systems of support. Martin and Deeqaifrah continue to stay connected with the university. Martin teaches as an adjunct faculty member and serves as a mentor teacher through his school district and university partner residency program. Deeqaifrah serves as a mentor on a federal grant that aims to recruit diverse special education teacher candidates.

Deeqaifrah became the first licensed Somali autism teacher in the state. It was important to her that other Somali men and women also earn a special education license, ensuring that students and the community receive education by those who look like them and have a deeper understanding of Somali cultural traditions and practices. Consequently, she provided consultation to Shelley, who wrote a federal personal preparation grant to fund scholarships for more individuals to earn licenses. As part of the grant, Deeqaifrah mentors cohorts of diverse special education teacher candidates. She is no longer the only Somali licensed teacher in special education in the state. By contributing to pathways for others to become teachers, she is creating more opportunities for all.

The university hired Martin to consult on the application of technology in coursework, lead a seminar on the application of technology for students with disabilities, and teach courses. His work at the university deepens his knowledge and skills as a special educator and enriches the competencies of the teacher candidates. Martin's course provides a comprehensive overview of special education and an introduction to the study of students ascribed the label of "exceptional." Through face-to-face and online teaching, Martin teaches the historical and legal background that informs present-day practices in special education. Martin presents the learning characteristics, abilities, and underlying needs of students with common characteristics across various disabilities, along with effective interventions in both general education and special education.

In addition, Martin serves as a mentor teacher in a residency program, a partnership between his school district and the university, which focuses on "recruiting, preparing, and retaining highly qualified teachers from underrepresented backgrounds who reflect the diverse student population of the district" (SPPS Urban Teacher Residency, n.d.). As a trained mentor teacher, Martin works closely with one resident from the beginning to the end of the school year. Martin coaches residents to use evidence-based strategies, grow and incubate cohesive teams, set routines and rituals for self-care, and establish strategies to last in the profession and persist in a challenging environment.

These professional connections provide sustained systems of support, an important component of persisting in this profession. According to Emmons (2010), social connections can be some of the most healing and fulfilling aspects of the profession that can help one build resilience. Martin's school colleagues, for example, welcomed him with open arms. As soon as the school year started, he had support from many veteran teachers. He also had an opportunity to co-teach with veteran general education teachers, who helped him develop his knowledge of grade-level standards and pedagogy. Martin recommends finding trustworthy allies who help prioritize the multiple responsibilities of teaching and who "have your back," especially during the first few years.

As a first-year special education resource teacher, Deeqaifrah relied on her family and work support system to provide constructive feedback, social emotional learning, and guidance on due process procedures and navigating collaboration teams within the school. Deeqaifrah's family served as a place to vent about her anxieties. At work, she found support in a district program facilitator and she had continued contact with Lynn and Shelley. Through these connections, Deeqaifrah was able to receive both informal and formal coaching. As a previous general education teacher, Deeqaifrah was skilled at classroom management and developed positive rapport with the students on her caseload. As a special education teacher, she continues to seek resources and networking to help further her support system. Deeqaifrah believes that using one's support system involves continuously learning and surrounding oneself with the experts in the field.

Lesson Five: Practice Self-Care

The job of special education teachers can be physically and mentally challenging. Martin sometimes feels that he is trying to hit a bull's-eye on a dartboard "while sticking his head outside a plane and bouncing on and off the pavement of a runway at 200 miles per hour"—an impossible task. He works long hours to finish paperwork. His arms and legs are scarred from students' behaviors. To persist as a special educator, remain happy, and make positive change for students and families, he realizes he must take time for daily self-care.

Martin practices self-care in a variety of ways. First, he identifies and capitalizes on his strengths. He regularly visualizes and embodies his most "resonated" or "authentic" self. According to Cuddy (2015), one's most authentic self "emerges through the experience of having full access to your values, traits, and strengths, and knowing that you can autonomously and sincerely express them through your actions and interactions" (p. 51). Cuddy recommends taking time to reflect and write down core values that are considered one's strengths. This list of core traits and values represent a picture of one's most resonated self.

Martin also uses running to calm his mind. He has run eight marathons all over the United States and racked up more than 2,700 training miles. As a runner, he uses "mantras," or positive self-talk, to keep moving forward. Research suggests that using positive affirmations can increase the ability to overcome challenging situations (Kaufman et al., 2018). Daily, Martin creates motivation mantras for himself that help him set small measurable goals and tackle his fears. He calls these his "wins" of the day.

When working with students, even the most challenging, he recognizes moments of celebration. Martin uses a journal to take very informal notes about instructional ideas, meetings, lessons, and accommodations that could be implemented later in the week. At the top of every page, he writes a mantra that helps him get through the day, such as "Stop and breathe," "Bring out your most resonated self today," "You are valuable," "You are whole," or "You are powerful." Martin shared that, on some days, while walking to the front door of the building, he pretends that he is wearing a suit of armor and uses more mantras: "My experience will guide me during tough times." He believes that utilizing daily mantras helps him establish boundaries for what is possible during the day.

Deeqaifrah admits that practicing self-care isn't easy. She plans intentionally to balance work, life, and school. She notices that self-care seems like the first thing dropped when pressures mount. She recommends establishing self-care habits in the first year of teaching, and adding self-care to priorities after due process, classroom management, and family.

MAINTAINING ONGOING CONNECTIONS TO INFLUENCE THE FIELD

We, Shelley, Martin, Deeqaifrah, and Lynn, persist and thrive independent of one another, yet share lived experiences as special educators. Through our involvement with the university and the teacher education program in which we first met, we inspire future educators to persist and thrive in a more diverse teacher preparation program. We strongly believe that our collaborations have contributed to preservice teacher candidates being exposed to real-life experiences and lessons that help them persist through graduation and thrive in the field.

Lynn and Shelley know that former students like Martin and Deeqaifrah help them remain current about issues in the field. They also learn about missed opportunities in teacher preparation and how to include content, discussions, and frameworks to help all educators grapple with critical topics related to bias, white privilege, and racism.

Together, we deepen our own individual special education knowledge and practice. We support each other, even when our confidence is rattled with feelings of doubt and disillusionment. Most important, nurturing these connections motivates us to persist. Together, we contribute to the social landscape of education in meaningful ways and challenge others to have honest and "tough" conversations about the topics we have raised in the chapter.

MY STORY: MARTIN ODIMA

My mother was a second-generation immigrant from the Philippines. My grandmother immigrated to America, started a business, and sent my mother to college. My father was an immigrant from a remote town in Nigeria. He worked hard to make enough money to immigrate to America and go to college. Growing up, my mother and father went hungry when there was not enough food. Until I was five years old, my mom, dad, and I lived in an apartment building known by some as the "Ghetto in the Sky"; most of the residents were very poor. I remember living around constant crime and poverty, and we owned little to nothing.

I was conflicted about my racial identity and never dreamed of being a teacher. It wasn't part of my parents' narrative and not a profession expected to bring wealth and pride to my family. Immigrants whose experiences were similar to my family traveled thousands of miles and left close friends and family members to come to a place where they had very few connections. They felt the need to assimilate to the dominant culture and navigated complicated systems. My family wanted me to be a lawyer or a doctor.

When I was a kid, I would roll my eyes when they would explain their story of coming to America. I was just trying to do my best to fit in and learn how to navigate the world as a skinny, black Filipino American kid in a predominantly white suburb. I was like a "social chameleon," trying to establish relationships with several different groups of people. I would find small ways to integrate myself into different social groups, sometimes awk-

wardly. I always felt a need to assimilate and navigate different social structures throughout my school career.

Selecting a career in special education was not my first choice. I felt a lot of pressure from my parents. I went to the state university and took premed classes. I put in an incredible number of hours of studying and seeking help from peers and tutors. However, I still struggled to pass courses and became depressed. During my sophomore year, I was deeply inspired by my African American history professor. He was the first black teacher I ever had. He challenged me in ways I'd never been challenged. His course was a paradigm shift and taught me about social and political movements, civil rights policies, and racial justice. He encouraged me to pursue my passions. Soon after, I decided to switch my major to psychology.

During college, I worked as a youth program counselor at an urban YMCA. The children I worked with had experiences like mine—many were minorities, some were first- or second-generation immigrants, and some had experienced poverty. A coworker at the YMCA told me about a job opening at a nearby public school, and I applied for it.

I can't imagine being anything but a special education teacher. By using the practices and strategies described in this chapter, I've been able to persist in a challenging profession. Being a special education teacher gives me an opportunity to express myself, be creative, and empower students to be proud of their identity no matter their racial, cultural, ethnic, or socioeconomic background. I attribute my core values of work in teaching to my family's history. After some deep reflection, I realize that educators have been leading me throughout my life. They challenged me in college, advocated for me when I worked as a paraprofessional, and welcomed me as a teacher.

MY STORY: DEEQAIFRAH HUSSEIN

My family fled the civil war in Somalia. We migrated to Yemen first, then to the United States. As a young immigrant child, I was thrown into a seventh-grade class where I didn't understand much of what was going on. Once we got here, it was very clear to all of us that the only way to succeed was through education. We worked hard, studied after school, always completed homework, and followed strict family expectations. We considered ourselves very lucky because there were families that never got the chance to flee the war. Once we got here, my family made sure we stayed on the right path. School was difficult because of the language barrier. There was one Somali girl in the whole school who was able to help from time to time; however, I wanted to learn more and understand my new world. I was immediately placed in English as a second language classes.

I had a teacher who was patient with me and inspired me to read books. I would read interesting short books that were easy to understand. She started with picture books and writing simple sentences. She challenged me with chapter books and asked me about what I learned daily. I strove to make her proud and challenged myself to read one chapter per week. I fell in love with reading and learning how to interact with my new peers. I was in a whole new world as I learned more about other subjects and was determined to excel in my other classes as well. My English teacher taught me early that with consistency, hard work, and patience, I could achieve anything I put my mind to.

Because I come from a family of educators, engineers, doctors, and business professionals, going straight to college was mandatory. There were no options for skipping a year or considering a major outside of biology, business, or electrical engineering. I wanted to become a pediatrician and majored in biology. I was living the American dream of going to college. There were unstated expectations about hard work. Working hard meant that grades could not be less than an A-minus, and if I had a B, I had to explain. Even though I was inspired by my mother, a medical doctor, biology was really not my strength. I soon realized that my passions did not align with the subject. My aunt, a special education teacher, mentored me and helped me find a teacher licensing program. I prepared to become a fourth–eighth grade general education teacher. Enrolling in that program was a gift. The program was for working professionals, which allowed me to work an eight-hour shift during the day and attend classes at night and on weekends.

After one year, I began work as a paid student teacher with mentors from the program and from my school district. While the first year of teaching is hard for many teachers, I truly enjoyed working with kids in an urban setting. During my first four years, I got to teach social studies and physical science. I also challenged myself to teach different content areas during summer school.

I enrolled in a university-based special education program after one of my children was diagnosed with autism and discovered firsthand the critical need for credentialed special educators. As a member of the Somali community, I understood families' feelings of vulnerability within the special education system and the cultural barriers preventing access to appropriate services. I wanted to help other families understand the systems and their rights. This led me to my path, first as an itinerant special education teacher serving students with Autism Spectrum Disorder (ASD) and Emotional and Behavior Disorders (EBD) across the district, and now as a special education director. My mission to serve and advocate for students and their families drives my ambition and helps me to get through tough and isolating times.

REFERENCES

Bettini, E., Jones, N. D., Brownell, M. T., Conroy, M., & Leite, W. (2018). Relationships between novices' social resources and workload manageability. *Journal of Special Education, 52*, 113–126.

Boe, E. E., & Cook, L. H. (2006). The chronic and increasing shortage of fully certified teachers in special and general education. *Exceptional Children, 72*(4), 443–460. Retrieved from https://doi.org/10.1177/001440290607200404

Bristol, T. (2015). Male teachers of color take a lesson from each other. *Phi Delta Kappan, 97*(2), 36–41.

Bristol, T. J., & Goings, R. B. (2018). Exploring the boundary-heightening experiences of black male teachers: Lessons for teacher education programs. *Journal of Teacher Education, 70*(1), 51–64.

Bryan, N., & Ford, D. Y. (2014). Recruiting and retaining black male teachers in gifted education. *Gifted Child Today, 37*(3), 156–161.

CAST. (2018). UDL and the learning brain. Retrieved from http://www.cast.org/binaries/content/assets/common/publications/articles/cast-udlandthebrain-20180321.pdf

Collaborative Urban Education Scholarship Program. (n.d.). Retrieved from https://education.stthomas.edu/admissionsandaid/tuition/scholarships/cue/

Covey, S. R. (2004). *The 7 habits of highly effective people: Restoring the character ethic*. New York, NY: Free Press.

Cuddy, A. (2015). *Presence: Bringing your boldest self to your biggest challenges*. New York, NY: Little, Brown and Company.

DiAngelo, R. (2011). White fragility. *International Journal of Critical Pedagogy, 3*(3) 54–70.

Educators 4 Excellence MN Teacher Policy Team (2015). *Closing Gaps: Diversifying Minnesota's Teacher Workforce*. Minneapolis, MN: Educators 4 Excellence.

Emmons, R. (2010), Why gratitude is good. *Greater Good Magazine: Science-Based Insights for a Meaningful Life*. Retrieved from https://greatergood.berkeley.edu/article/item/why_gratitude_is_good

Gargiulo, R. M., & Bouck, E. C. (2018). *Special education in contemporary society: An introduction to exceptionality* (6th ed). Thousand Oaks, CA: Sage Publications.

Goings, R. B. (2015). The lion tells his side of the (counter)story: A black male educator's autoethnographic account. *Journal of African American Males in Education, 6*(1), 91–105.

Ingersoll, R., & May, H. (2011). Recruitment retention and the minority teacher shortage. Consortium for Policy Research in Education (CPRE) Research Report #RR-69, 23. Retrieved November 2017, from https://www.cpre.org/sites/default/files/researchreport/1221_minorityteachershortagereportrr69septfinal.pdf

Jackson, I., & Knight-Manuel, M. (2018). "Color does not equal consciousness": Educators of color learning to enact a sociopolitical consciousness. *Journal of Teacher Education.* Advance online publication. doi:10.1177/0022487118783189

Kaufman, K., Glass, C., & Pineau, T. (2018). Performance applications beyond sport. In K. Kaufman, C. Glass, & T. Pineau (Eds.), *Mindful Sport Performance Enhancement: Mental Training for Athletes and Coaches* (pp. 205–219). Washington, DC: American Psychological Association.

National Coalition on Personnel Shortages in Special Education. (2014). *Special education personnel shortages fact sheet*. Retrieved from http://specialedshortages.org/wp-content/uploads/2014/03/NCPSSERS-Fact-Sheet.pdf

Stempien, L. R., & Loeb, R. C. (2002). Differences in job satisfaction between general education and special education teachers: Implications for retention. *Remedial and Special Education, 23*(5), 258–267. https://doi.org/10.1177/07419325020230050101

Sanchez, J. (2015). *Minnesota teachers of color: Modernizing our teacher workforce*. St. Paul, MN: Minnesota Education Equity Partnership.

SPPS Urban Teacher Residency (SUTR). (n.d.). Retrieved from https://www.spps.org/SUTR

Stempien, L. R., & Loeb, R. C. (2002). Differences in job satisfaction between general education and special education teachers: Implications for retention. *Remedial and Special Education, 23*(5), 258–267. https://doi.org/10.1177/07419325020230050101

Villegas, A., and Irvine, J. (2010). Diversifying the teaching force: An examination of major arguments. *The Urban Review, 42*(175–192), 180. Retrieved from http://link.springer.com/article/10.1007%2Fs11256-010-0150-1

US Department of Education. (2015-2016). *Teacher Shortage Areas Nationwide Listing 1990–1991 through 2015–2016*. Retrieved from https://www2.ed.gov/about/offices/list/ope/pol/tsa.pdf

Chapter Four

Rowing Together in the Same Direction

How Entwined Symbiosis Empowers Teachers at All Levels to Embrace Culturally Responsive Teaching

Katharine Covino, Garrett Zecker, and Hannah M. Britten

There are few professions as demanding as teaching. To be a teacher is to serve an ascetic vocation or a calling. So why (and how) do teachers persist and thrive in this all-consuming profession? How are they able to remain true to their principles and philosophies in a time of ever-increasing expectations and ever-encroaching restrictions? One answer to this question resides in the powerful and productive relationships that exist between classroom teachers and university instructors. By strategically supporting each other and by working together to "raise up" the next generation of teachers, educators working at divergent levels can collaboratively establish dynamic and empowering relationships that can help them pursue personal, professional, and political goals.

While partnerships can be used to support any number of pedagogic aspirations, the most crucial focus for education in the globalized twenty-first century is culturally responsive teaching (Gay, 2000). Culturally responsive teaching is the foundation of preservice teachers' work with diverse learners. Gay (2000) describes culturally responsive teaching as the "cultural knowledge, prior experiences, frames of reference, and performance styles of ethnically diverse students to make learning encounters more relevant to and effective for them. It teaches to and through the strengths of these students. It is culturally validating and affirming" (p. 29).

Novice teachers' understanding of culturally responsive teaching supports all students' literacy learning and development, reading comprehension, and writing abilities, and some scholars (e.g., Gee, 2000) extend the concept of culturally responsive teaching to literacy learning. Since Heath's (1982) groundbreaking study, educators have known about the powerful linkages that exist between home learning and school literacy learning; specifically, "how poverty, discrimination, exploitation, anti-immigrant sentiment, language ideologies, and educational and social policies" (Gutierrez, 2008, p. 149) can negatively affect children's experiences in school.

It is now more crucial than ever that classroom teachers and university instructors draw upon each other's experiences and expertise to train preservice teachers to support students from culturally and linguistically diverse backgrounds (Jiménez, 2004). Building from students' funds of knowledge (Moll et al., 1992) and drawing their rich cultural intelligence and linguistic capital into the curriculum, teacher educators and veteran teachers can work together to educate preservice teachers to think more expansively and inclusively—to broaden and hybridize their understanding of literacy (Mills, 2010). The fundamental importance of this work is the creation of equity and accessibility through the dynamic practice of literacies in and out of schools (Freire, 1970).

This chapter explores culturally responsive teaching as it relates to literacy learning from three distinct yet overlapping perspectives: (1) a university instructor (Katharine) shares her thoughts on educating middle and secondary English teachers and helping them consider ways of building bridges between home and school, therefore redefining literacy; (2) a veteran high school English teacher (Garrett), committed to lifelong service of underserved, marginalized, urban English language learners (ELLs), considers his dual roles as a supervising practitioner and a classroom teacher in his own right; and (3) a newly licensed high school English teacher (Hannah) looks back to her recent pedagogic training and forward (with both apprehension and hope) to her daily struggles in her own newly acquired classroom.

Together, we make clear that only by rowing together in the same direction can we shelter ourselves from the prevailing winds that seek to couple minority status with failure. Drawing on more than forty years of combined teaching experience, we share how our *entwined symbiosis*—our practice of sharing and working to fulfill our own pedagogical philosophies and goals related to culturally responsive teaching—becomes mutually gratifying and endlessly sustaining.

ENTWINED SYMBIOSIS: A NEW MODEL

Most teachers working in today's schools recognize that as each year passes, the student population they serve becomes increasingly multilingual and diverse (National Center for Education Statistics, 2019). While research in the field has moved past the trend that labels such learners as "deprived" or "deficient," educators at all levels need to maintain practices that empower, rather than denigrate, the students in their classrooms (Agar, 2006). As high-stakes accountability tests continue to steer top-down mandates, the weight of national influence on local educational policy becomes heavier and more burdensome. A hard and honest look reveals just how frequently such measures are weaponized to close schools, redistrict administrators, or end teachers' careers (Putnam, 2015).

The twenty-first-century urban high school is a melting pot of both intellectual dynamism and cultural pluralism. Public schools often redesign their mission to be student-led. This shift is not only to stem the tide of students whose families opt for charter schools but also to reimagine what it means to educate students for the future (Johnston, 2019). Even smaller schools, once considered stalwart bellwethers against larger urban schools in funding and opportunities, are feeling the effects of what urban environments offer. Rural and suburban political leaders worry that they will not be able to compete with large urban centers and name the exodus from suburban and rural schools a "brain drain"; most students and families will never return to the smaller environment (Dreher, 2018).

Too often, the weight of the pressures of migration and accountability fall disproportionately on the shoulders of novice teachers. Eager for their first jobs, these young, inexperienced educators eagerly accept positions at high-need, underfunded schools where turnover is high and burnout is rampant. The US Department of Labor reported that an average of eighty-three out of every ten thousand public educators quit the profession in the first ten months of 2018, a record high since these figures began being compiled in 2001 when states began crushing unions, tying test data to teacher performance and school budgets, and standardizing homogeneous expectations (Hackman & Morath, 2018).

Alone in their classrooms, with far too much riding on student performance, novice teachers face a grim choice: do they quit, throw up their hands in despair, or take on the cloak of the "white savior" and "fix . . . communities and their members so that they match normative views and practices" (Gutierrez, 2008, p. 151)? Given these many external demands and stressors, it is a dark temptation for brand-new teachers to come to view student differences in learning as deficits in ability (Michaels, 1981). With few positive outcomes, new teachers are far too often set up to fail.

What can be done to help avert this problematic eventuality? In this time of challenging nationalized imperatives, how can English teachers work together to sustain each other and strengthen their deep commitment to practices that embrace the richness and power of the cultural and linguistic diversity of their students (Mills, 2010)? How can different generations of teachers working in different spheres build sustainable alliances that can withstand the building power of external forces?

One answer resides in a model of dynamic and supportive collaborative partnership—what this chapter refers to as entwined symbiosis. In this model, university instructors, supervising practitioners, and novice teachers work with and through each other to ensure that each remains true to the central mission of culturally responsive teaching, which is the thoughtful inclusion and authentic valuation of social and cultural differences at all levels of teaching. Within this model (as in the case illustrated in this chapter), a local urban high school and the surrounding community serve as focal points of connection for the university professor, the supervising practitioner, and the novice teacher.

Working together for the betterment of students, the university professor, supervising practitioner, and novice teacher are connected to their counterparts within the larger world of state and national research, mandates, and reform related to English education. The model draws on the strengths, talents, and experiences of teachers at divergent levels. It also calls into play a host of other educational resources and supports, including community centers, museums, and family outreach clinics. Built on years of commitment and trust, each plays a role in service of the others—as a mentor, a model, or a novice practitioner of culturally responsive teaching. At its core, entwined symbiosis represents educators engaging in continual reflection, communication, and guidance with and for each other. Acting both individually and in concert, they create a united foundation—stronger and more sustainable for its far-reaching network of deep-sunk roots. It is a system built over time to sustain best practice.

THE UNIVERSITY INSTRUCTOR: MENTORING CULTURALLY RESPONSIVE TEACHERS

Teaching and mentoring future English teachers are the primary responsibilities of a university professor specializing in secondary English education. Although seemingly self-evident, this task takes on new meaning within the entwined symbiosis model. The model alters the way that university professors design, implement, and assess their courses. In this model, it is not just the university, or even the state, that drives the direction of the coursework. The local secondary school stands as a third coequal partner.

The decision to give equivalent weight to the needs of the supervising practitioner and his students differs from current practice. No longer can university professors create their courses in a vacuum. No longer will lack of alignment between the university classroom and the secondary classroom come at the cost of artificial and intrusive lessons force-fed to high school students (Covino, 2019). That is not to say that university professors relinquish all responsibility, but rather, their responsibilities shift. Still tasked with the difficult charge of raising up the next generation of culturally responsive teachers, university instructors must identify critical areas of scholarship that relate to culturally responsive pedagogy. But, in this model, they must do so in concert with the supervising practitioners.

Working together, university professors and secondary classroom educators create opportunities for novice teacher teachers to engage in *praxis* (the intersection of theory and practice) that meet the needs of the state, the university, the partner schools, and the communities (Freire, 1970, p. 84). This is not easy work. Given the focus on culturally responsive teaching, there are two critical themes that emerge from academic writing and scholarship that form the backbone for the synergistic course redesign: (1) bridging the gap between home and school (Moll et al., 1992) and (2) redefining literacy as "literacies" (Gee, 2000; Gutierrez, 2008). Having identified these central goals, the university professor works in tandem with the supervising practitioner to craft essential questions, objectives, activities, and assessments that address these topics in ways that model culturally responsive teaching and that support the secondary students, their families, and the surrounding community.

Culturally responsive teaching is not possible if novice teachers do not know their students. Therefore, one of the most central goals of any English methods course must be educating novice teachers to learn more about their students, their students' families, and the larger community. Many strategies entwine the shared goals of university professors and supervising practitioners while also helping novice teachers make connections between home and school.

For example, inexperienced teachers often struggle to establish classroom norms. Frequently, their struggle reflects their lack of knowledge about their students' identities and the culture of the school. An assessment that asks these teachers to consider contextual factors when establishing classroom norms represents a remedy that intermarries the needs of novice teacher, secondary school students, supervising practitioner, and university professor. Success on such an assessment would demand that novice teachers use information about the learning/teaching context and individual student differences to set learning goals, plan instruction, and assess learning in ways that reflect their growing knowledge of their students, the school, and the community.

Partnering with a supervising practitioner to teach and evaluate this university-level assessment would further deepen and authenticate the entwined symbiosis model. Driven by the shared goal of developing a "more sophisticated understanding of the student, his family, and his social world" (Moll et al., 1992, p. 137), the university professor, the supervising practitioner, and novice teacher each become stakeholders in a real-world, on-the-ground project that furthers their commitment to bridging the gap between home and school through the practice of culturally responsive teaching.

THE VETERAN TEACHER AND SUPERVISING PRACTITIONER: MODELING CULTURALLY RESPONSIVE TEACHING

In myriad ways, educators' work in urban schools represents the vanguard of the future of education. Many innovative achievements by urban high schools are precisely the result of their foundational diversity teamed with the dynamic foundations that exist in the collaborative partnership between university professor, the supervising practitioner, the novice teacher, and the community as a whole.

The unique role of the supervising practitioner at the urban high school is specifically to examine the roles and responsibilities of the preservice teacher's program while functioning as a mentor of the profession. The supervising practitioner also upholds expectations of the local secondary school and community (including their local and state requirements of student performance) and perhaps most uniquely, approaches these expectations differently to enrich the novice teacher's access to the culture and climate of the school and student body.

There is no question that the supervising practitioner and university professor immediately recognize that one of the novice teacher's main concerns is the content itself. The challenge comes in executing the content while addressing the primary cultural, linguistic, and sociopolitical needs of the students while recognizing their place in the community. Without exception, the delicate balance of the needs of the three professionals working in tandem has propelled novice teachers to have a tendency toward "emphasizing mandated and tested content and to view—even define—content areas in relation to parameters set by mandated programs, rather than the broader domains of knowledge that those programs hypothetically sought to address;" that is, preservice teachers must meet the training and performance requirements of the university and the state curriculum requirements of the host school (Anderson & Stillman, 2011, p. 450).

However, it does not take long for novice teachers to recognize how "observations alone did not help them understand how they could strategically adapt mandated curricula to meet students' needs authentically, responsively, and engagingly"; this process only leads to the "disengagement that often accompanie(s) scripted teaching" (Anderson & Stillman, 2011, p. 450). To complicate matters more, second language learners face even more hurdles to the content in these areas.

The entwined symbiosis model allows the supervising practitioner to use many tools to assist their novice teachers and university supervisors in working together with the local secondary school and community not only to meet the basic requirements of all of the various institutions at work in training them for the field but also to fuel exciting engagement and innovation in their students, classroom, and community.

To maximize the effectiveness of a novice teacher's impact on their students, it is the supervising practitioner's responsibility to educate the novice teacher on the culture and climate of the school and the needs of ELLs in their classrooms. Together, the supervising practitioner and the novice teacher formulate innovative approaches for the students, the required content of their university program, and the state curriculum. Since consciousness of race and language should and do characterize the novice teacher's credential program and the needs of the students, the supervising practitioner helps the novice teacher recognize that "classes should be structured to replace test requirements for language competency requirements" (Murai et al., 2019, p. 79).

Additionally, the novice teacher and supervising practitioner examine the ways that "sociohistoric roots, local community events, and community members' cultures shaped how discussants often reproduced a white normalized gaze on difference and at times ignored thornier issues of structural inequities" when discussing the generally accepted approaches to reading and writing (Athanases, 2006, p. 17). In this way, the university professor and the supervising practitioner both play a role in modeling innovative pedagogy that recognizes and values the cultural and linguistic identities of their students.

THE NOVICE TEACHER:
PRACTICING CULTURALLY RESPONSIVE TEACHING

The novice teacher ebbs and flows alongside their mentors and support systems. While they do not encroach upon each other, the combined wisdom of each guides the others forward. All new educators must look back on their recent pedagogic training while remaining reflective and insightful of their student's preferences, attitudes, behaviors, backgrounds, and personalities. With the wisdom shared by their university professors and the newly gained insights from their supervising practitioner, a novice teacher may feel confident and courageous entering the first phase of their career.

The preservice teacher is in a constant and consistent state of chaos and is ever searching for new ideas and improved pedagogical theories. As novice teachers take their first steps, they will look in every possible direction through a whirlwind of supports, advice, and mentors, back to their pedagogical training and forward toward the culture and climate of their urban school. Entwined symbiosis outlines such a dance, marked by the elements noted in the following sections.

Constructing a classroom environment requires a great deal of forethought and planning, especially for novice educators. The atmosphere of a classroom directly affects students' moods and comfort levels. Many high school age students develop "school phobia," a fear or strong distaste of going to school. While some students develop this problem because of their fluctuating grades, others may have social anxiety, learning disabilities, and many other factors that they are struggling to deal with. Throughout the student teaching experience, the preservice teacher will feel as if they are walking a tightrope with no insight into what is to come next.

As the supervising practitioner and university professor warned, maintaining a classroom atmosphere equipped with rules and routines is arguably the most difficult hurdle the new teacher will overcome. Thus, as they walk blindly forward one foot in front of the other, the preservice teacher will rely on the combined wisdom of the entwined symbiosis model for guidance. Not only is the classroom the culmination of where learning takes place, but it houses the joining of different personalities, backgrounds, ideologies, and cultures five times over (depending on how many classes in one school day).

As the novice teacher transitions from their role as student teacher to leading their own classroom, they must remain cognizant of their university professor's mentoring, their supervising practitioner's modeling, the community, their pedagogical training, and, now, make it their own (Lane, Menzies, Bruhn, & Crnobori, M., 2010). Whether a student's outlook on learning is negative or positive directly correlates with the student's academic achievement.

When establishing a classroom environment it is crucial to remember this simple fact, as the entwined symbiosis model represents: Educators must embody continual reflection, communication, and guidance. This reflection and guidance continue when constructing classroom norms and routines. As the university professor previously mentioned, the contextual factors of a class must reflect and represent the contextual factors of the school and the student body.

Educators must always remain hyperaware of their students' performance in school, but moreover, must remain aware of the lives of their students outside of the classroom. Such vigilance and awareness are achievable (even for the novice teacher) because of the connections and conversations that exist in the entwined symbiosis model. If a student has set their attitude against learning, the teacher must present an alternative emotion.

As the supervising practitioner aids and eases the novice teacher into the climate and culture of the school, the university professor highlights the significance of such contextual factors and provides pedagogical strategies for how to teach such a student body. The novice teacher must then become hyperaware of the school's subgroups and behaviors. With the coming together of diverse cultures, it is the educator's responsibility to remain dynamic and flexible so that they may reach each student. In order to achieve such culturally responsive teaching, a bottom-up or backward design approach can be helpful.

WORKING TOGETHER TO DISRUPT THE SYSTEM

Culturally responsive teaching, as pedagogy, empowers students on all levels by building on their knowledge and experiences to deepen teaching and social growth. Engaging students in learning tasks that not only have cultural significance but also expose unjust practices empowers students to challenge the status quo. Thus, the tenets of culturally responsive teaching closely align with teaching for social justice (Gutstein, 2003).

Culturally responsive teaching may *begin* in the classroom, but it goes much further, correlating with lifelong learning. Culturally responsive teaching promotes and supplies opportunities for students and educators of all ages to "learn about and legitimize the cultural heritages of themselves and others, while using multicultural curricular materials to explicitly connect culture" (Walter, 2018, p. 25) to the content and strategic activities of the lesson, thus representing and including all.

Teachers of disadvantaged youth and others must aim to help students to develop their own identity and voice within the learning community. Using their recent pedagogical research gained via their university professor and sustained by their supervising practitioner, the novice teacher is continuously pushing boundaries and looking for the next pedagogical practice. All novice teachers must observe as many teaching styles and pedagogical practices possible.

When teaching at an urban school it is important to explain to the students not only what they are learning but why they are learning it. Without the meta-cognitive buy-in, students will dismiss and demote all activities presented to them. It is through exposure and the analysis of those with experience that new educators gain insight. This stands as an applied example of entwined symbiosis, where each individual supports and upholds the teaching and learning of the others.

When teaching at an urban public school especially, it is crucial to integrate students' cultural and social capital into all goals (in class and individually). It is the responsibility of the instructor to ensure that all students set academic and personal goals in a meaningful context that resonates with them (Jensen, 2013). When student teaching, the university professors will call upon their students to research the local school's demographics and sub-demographics, described as contextual factors that shape student learning. Doing so will allow the novice teacher to truly understand where they are teaching and who they are teaching. Before a teacher can teach, they must first understand who it is they are teaching (Larson et al., 2018).

Novice teachers benefit a great deal from the continuing support and encouragement of their university professors and supervisors. Such mentors continue to hold high standards for pedagogy and are committed to researching literacy teaching and learning. Such standards encourage young educators to perfect their pedagogy and pursue their passions. Educators have a duty to disrupt a broken system. By listening and learning from their mentor veterans, any novice teacher will be better off and will be more equipped to do just that.

REFERENCES

Agar, M. (2006). Culture: Can you take it anywhere? *International Journal of Qualitative Methods, 5*(2), 3–12.

Anderson, L., & Stillman, J. (2011). Student teaching for a specialized view of professional practice? Opportunities to learn in and for urban, high-needs schools. *Journal of Teacher Education, 62*(5), pp. 446+. *Expanded Academic ASAP*. Retrieved from http://link.galegroup.com/apps/doc/A271664903/EAIM?u=mlin_b_bpublic&sid=EAIM&xid=c4d3ca39

Athanases, S. Z. (2006). Deepening teacher knowledge of multicultural literature through a university-schools partnership. *Multicultural Education, 13*(4), 17. *Expanded Academic ASAP*. Retrieved from http://link.galegroup.com/apps/doc/A148768042/EAIM?u=mlin_b_bpublic&sid=EAIM&xid=21c9462d

Covino, K. (2019). "It's just not what I thought it would be": Teacher candidates navigating tensions in identity. In H. L. Hallman, K. Pastore-Capuana, & D. L. Pasternak (Eds.), *Possibilities, challenges, and changes in English teacher education today—Exploring identity and professionalization* (pp. 21–35). Lanham, MD: Rowman & Littlefield.

Dreher, A. (2018). Can innovative rural schools stem the urban bleed? *T74 Newsletter*. Retrieved from http://www.the74million.org/article/can-innovative-rural-schools-stem-the-urban-bleed-and-reseed-middle-america

Freire, P. (1970). *Pedagogy of the oppressed*. New York, NY: Seabury Press.

Gay, G. (2000). *Culturally responsive teaching: Theory, research, and practice*. New York, NY: Teachers College Press.

Gee, J. P. (2000). Identity as an analytic lens for research in education. *Review of Research in Education, 25*, 99–125.

Gutierrez, K. (2008). Developing a sociocritical literacy in the third space. *Reading Research Quarterly, 43*(2), 148–164.

Gutstein, E. (2003). Teaching and learning mathematics for social justice in an urban, Latino school. *Journal for Research in Mathematics Education, 34*, 37–73. doi:10.2307/30034699

Hackman, M., & Morath, E. (2018, December 29). Teachers quit jobs at highest rate on record. *Wall Street Journal Eastern Edition*, A3(NA). Retrieved from http://link.galegroup.com.ezproxy.bpl.org/apps/doc/A567922154/AONE?u=mlin_b_bpublic&sid=AONE&xid=59ad6f66

Heath, S. B. (1982). What no bedtime story means. *Language in Society, 11*, 49–76.

Jensen, E. (2010). *Teaching with poverty in mind: What being poor does to kids' brains and what schools can do about it.* Alexandria, VA: ASCD.

Jensen, E. (2013). *Engaging students with poverty in mind: Practical strategies for raising achievement.* Alexandria, VA: ASCD.

Jiménez, R. T. (2004). Literacy and identity development in Latina/o students. In R. B. Ruddell & N. J. Unrau (Eds.), *Theoretical models and processes of reading* (pp. 210–239). Newark, DE: International Reading Association.

Johnston, R. (2019, April 5). Dallas schools are winning back students with new focus on innovation. *EdScoop.* Retrieved from http://edscoop.com/dallas-schools-are-winning-back-students-with-new-focus-on-steam/

Lane, K. L., Menzies, H. M., Bruhn, A. L., & Crnobori, M. (2010). *Managing challenging behaviors in schools: Research-based strategies that work.* New York: Guilford Press.

Larson, K. E., Pas, E. T., Bradshaw, C. P., Rosenberg, M. S., Day-Vines, N. L., & Gregory, A. (2018). Examining how proactive management and culturally responsive teaching relate to student behavior: Implications for measurement and practice. *School Psychology Review, 47*(2), 153–166.

Michaels, S. (1981). "Sharing time": Children's narrative styles and differential access to literacy. *Language in Society, 10*(3), 423–442.

Mills, K. A. (2010). A review of the "digital turn" in the New Literacy Studies. *Review of Educational Research, 80*(2), 246–271.

Moll, L. C., Amanti, C., Neff, D., & Gonzalez, N. (1992). Funds of knowledge for teaching: Using a qualitative approach to connect homes and classrooms. *Theory into Practice, 31*(2), 132–141.

Murai, H., Berta-Ávila, M., & Figueróa-Ramírez, K. (2019). Reflections and lessons learned. *Teacher Education Quarterly, 46*(1), pp. 79–85.

National Center for Education Statistics (2019). The condition of education: English language learners in public schools. Retrieved October 2019, from https://nces.ed.gov/programs/coe/indicator_cgf.asp

Putnam, R. D. (2015). *Our kids.* New York, NY: Simon and Schuster.

Walter, J. S. (2018). Global perspectives: Making the shift from multiculturalism to culturally responsive teaching. *General Music Today, 31*(2), 24–28.

II

Political Landscapes

Chapter Five

Ongoing Transformation

Exploring the Chronologies of Becoming a Teacher

Margaret Flynn and Heidi L. Hallman

Developing as a teacher inherently invites a process of socialization yet is also influenced by one's history and background. Britzman (1991) argues that this process of teacher socialization is influenced by *chronologies*. The concept of chronologies conveys a simultaneity of time, place, events, and the meanings that we give to them (Britzman, 1991, p. 55). Acknowledging that teachers are influenced by at least four chronologies during the process of becoming teachers, Britzman notes that each chronology makes available a different range of voices and discourses. In this chapter, one teacher, Margaret, traces these chronologies within the narratives she presents. Showing her movement from beginning teacher to in-service teacher highlights not only the competence required in being a teacher, but also the emotional strength and resilience needed to persevere in the profession.

Britzman's (1991) work acknowledges that teachers bring the first chronology with them, which is their educational biography and the synthesis they have created to make sense of the rules that govern schools, the nature of knowing, and the purpose of schooling. The second chronology involves teachers' experiences in the university and in teacher education. The third chronology is the student teaching/intensive field experience, where Britzman argues that teachers begin to become privy to aspects of teachers' worlds and departmental politics, and the fourth chronology begins when the teacher becomes a new, first-year teacher. The fourth chronology invites a teacher's newfound contemplation and understanding of the influences of "the school system, students, the teacher union, the community, public policy, professional organizations, and the cumulative experience of their classroom lives" (p. 56).

In this chapter, we add a fifth chronology to underscore the process of continual renewal that teachers must undertake in order to reinvigorate their practice. We call the fifth chronology one of transformation, a theme that highlights moving forward in one's career and pushing oneself to develop new interests and competencies. It is through the pathway of these chronologies that one can see themes of how teachers persist—how teachers sustain their energy and investment in the teaching profession.

Through examining Margaret's experiences, this chapter grapples with the following question: How can beginning teachers recognize this early on in teacher education without dismay? Although facing complexity in teaching and in schooling may seem somewhat daunting, we see that this complexity may present a possibility for agency, and teachers' agency gives rise to the idea that all teachers are capable of rethinking their prior assumptions and moving toward productive solutions. Possessing agency, teachers are always capable of questioning normative discourses at work.

Margaret's narratives also relate to her development as a social justice–oriented teacher. We draw our definition of social justice–oriented teaching from Boyd's (2017) work; Boyd claims that "teaching is itself a form of activism that allows for the realization of social justice both in *how* and *what* educators teach their students" (p. 7). The *how* and *what* aspects of teaching for social justice push teachers to recognize not only that social inequities and injustices exist but also that teachers must act for social change. Teaching and learning that is committed to social justice and equity must emphasize that school is about students' lives as well as about a particular subject area. We see this orientation throughout Margaret's commitment to the teaching profession.

Our relationship began with a commitment to equity. Heidi had planned a project within her teacher education program that asked preservice teachers to work with homeless youth in an after-school tutoring program. Margaret, a preservice teacher in the program at the time, was one of the first beginning teachers to volunteer. Heidi remembers Margaret's commitment to the program, even in its fledgling stages. After ten years of sustaining the program, Heidi still reflects on Margaret's enthusiasm for working with youth. Now, the chapter moves into the narratives that depict the particulars about Margaret's journey.

THE FIRST CHRONOLOGY: ONE'S BIOGRAPHY

Teachers bring the first chronology with them, which is their educational biography and the synthesis they have created to make sense of the rules that govern schools, the nature of knowing, and the purpose of schooling. In the following narrative, Margaret details how her family influenced her pursuit of a career in education. Heidi and Margaret are first united in this chronology when Margaret speaks of her work volunteering at Family Promise, a program that serves homeless families:

I come from a long line of public servants, specifically teachers. My extended family has in some capacity pursued a calling to serve the public communities that matter most to them. My father worked for thirty years in public administration, my mother served as the union representative at the elementary school where she taught for more than twenty years, and my grandmother, grandfather, aunts, uncles, cousins, and siblings have all made serving others, getting involved, and championing change the center of their work.

In addition, the fight and drive for fair labor is deeply rooted in my family's history. My great-grandfather, after immigrating from Sicily in 1910, joined the Bricklayer's Union of Chicago—a union that remains the oldest, continuously operating trade union in North America. In this way, my sense of self-advocacy and passion for work that directly influences my community runs in my blood.

Growing up, conversations at the dinner table concentrated on social issues. My parents made it a priority to expose my brothers and me to social movements and the political process early in life. I remember as a seventh grader watching my older brother, Joey, make picket signs to protest the war in Iraq. My parents did not lecture him on the impossibility that his involvement as a fifteen-year-old was going to make a difference. They did not push their views on him, hoping he would become a carbon copy of their political opinions.

Instead, they too stood up. They asked questions and shared history of meetings, marches, protests, and violence. Yes, they cautioned his action, but they celebrated more his curiosity to resist. My parents' own enthusiasm for political activism grounded me as a child in an essential value: that you did not always need a law or governmental policy to make your community better. They said yes to charitable work on weekends. They actively supported our schools, organized coat drives, and donated energy to nonprofit organizations. And as many times as I bemoaned waking up early to help, I knew the work was important.

So, in high school I called upon my family's belief in making a positive change on a community and became the copresident of the recycling club. As sixteen-year-olds, my copresident and I organized a schoolwide initiative to bring recycling facilities to our school. Seeing those red recycling bins in each classroom a year later made a lasting impact on my teenage heart.

I continued my work for the greater good in college, where I volunteered regularly at Family Promise, tutoring and mentoring children whose families were experiencing homelessness. There, my tolerance and awareness sharp-

ened and encouraged me to have a responsibility in supporting my community on a daily basis.

As a twenty-year-old I marched for educational funding, chanted for protection of women's rights, rallied friends and family to write letters to community members and government officials to support a historic and innovative amendment in Colorado, and demanded things change in the district I teach. My commitment and zeal to be a change agent remains resolute. In fact, my passion to help create a more just and fair educational system has buoyed my persistence to stay in the classroom.

Even after six years, the teaching workload does not scare me. I am not daunted by the endless responsibilities of teachers today. I am tired, yes, but I continue to get involved and go first because I believe in modeling bravery and risk-taking for my students. I cannot become inert with despair when things seem wrong. If I want my students to believe, hope, and achieve, I know I have to as well. This is the belief I carry because my family carried it first.

One of the ways that people understand themselves and how others perceive them is through the stories they tell of interactions with one another. Interactions with family and one's biography play a central role in identity formation. Margaret's narrative describes how her present is intermingled with stories of her past—stories of growing up, stories of her justice-oriented work in college, and even stories of her family members of past generations.

In Margaret's recounting, these stories act as *counterstories* (Yosso, 2006). Yosso describes the purpose of counterstories as having four functions: to "build community with those at the margins," to "challenge the perceived wisdom of those at society's center," to "nurture community wealth, memory, and resistance," and to "facilitate transformation in education" (pp. 14–15). Serving others and becoming active in taking a stance on social issues becomes a valued counterstory for Margaret—something that she pursued as a unique and important stance. Margaret, throughout this narrative, identifies the message of her biography as one that instilled what she names an "essential value": you do not always need a law or governmental policy to make your community better. This agentive statement equips Margaret with a vibrancy needed to be a change agent, something that, in regard to teaching, emerges next in her teacher education and student teaching experience.

THE SECOND AND THIRD CHRONOLOGIES: TEACHER EXPERIENCES IN TEACHER EDUCATION/STUDENT TEACHING

The second chronology involves teachers' experiences in the university and teacher education, while the third chronology details the significance of the student teaching/internship experience. In the following narrative, Margaret highlights the significance of the second and third chronologies. This chronology continues to unite Heidi and Margaret; Heidi was Margaret's faculty advisor in her teacher education program:

I put my "go first" mentality on the line during my student teaching internship as a fifth-year master's student at my university. At that time, my university's school of education program was designed to allow students the opportunity to earn a bachelor of science degree in education along with a master's degree in curriculum and instruction in just five years.

The fifth year was especially innovative because it required graduate coursework while also calling for students to complete two different student teaching placements. This meant that you were teaching full-time as a teacher intern and going to graduate school in the evenings. For someone like me, this was convenient rather than intimidating. My intent to teach in the first place was to become a partner in the process of public education. So, when I found out about my university's Professional Development Schools (PDS) Alliance program I knew I would forgo the traditional suburban setting of two student teaching places and apply to the PDS program.

The idea of being part of one collaborative professional community that centered on the ultimate goal of improving education for a diverse group of children sparked my intention of being a change agent in public education. For me, this awareness and solution-oriented model to teaching was revolutionary. For decades, my dream classroom consisted of twenty eager learners, with each of whom I established meaningful connections daily. My dream life as a teacher was fair, supportive, and sustainable and my students returned to the same seats in the same classroom to share their achievements with me, still Miss Flynn to them.

The PDS program shifted this fantasy into a more tangible, less romanticized image of public education. I was naive to think that my passion for teaching and educational experience at a top-ten teaching program were sufficient. I knew that Argentine Middle School, where I would spend my PDS teaching internship, had a student population that was far different from my own educational experience.

What I did not know was what this meant for me, the teacher. This was not the fault of the PDS program. The program required school visits and a host of teacher/student observations prior to teaching. However, the day-to-day grind, the mistakes, the assumptions, the teacher-fantasies that I lived in, could not be taught through graphic organizers and discussion posts.

To get to know my students and their needs, I had to be aware of who I was teaching. This awareness often meant changing my perspective. I needed to feel the rawness of teaching in an environment I never experienced as a student. I needed to listen more than instruct. It was day one of my profes-

sional development at Argentine Middle School that drove home this notion best.

Neither I nor the other four PDS interns in my cohort lived in the Argentine school community, so day one of our professional development was spent getting to know the culture and socioeconomic background of the community outside the historic brick building where we would soon teach. We took a bus around each corner and over every steep hill of the neighborhood. Our school assistant principal, who lived in the community, was our tour guide. She told stories, weighed in on issues, and celebrated the many faces of Argentine's community. We saw where students walked, waited for the bus, hung out after school, bought groceries, and gathered on the weekends. We ate lunch at a neighborhood favorite, shared experiences, and changed perceptions.

This was a monumental day for me in my career as a teacher because it was so unorthodox. The PDS program at Argentine Middle School dusted off the hidden reality of teaching and allowed the very people themselves into the school community space. Argentine knew that culture, politics, history, and socioeconomic class were prominent factors we starry-eyed and unaware "dreamers" were going to face head-on. This school made sure we were aware and ready of this reality on day one.

To this day, no teaching course or professional development conference has reinforced this critical need for awareness and advocacy quite as effectively. From that first experience bumping over potholes on a school bus, I knew politics and activism were going to be a major influencer in my career as a teacher.

Margaret writes that her desire to become a teacher was to become a partner in public education. In her narrative, she writes about how this theory of partnership might move into practice. Through her university's PDS program, Margaret develops her practice. She not only links themes of being a change agent in public education with the PDS program but also connects themes of her own growth as an educator with the PDS experience.

Research on PDS programs (Connor & Killmer, 2001; Sandholtz and Wasserman, 2001) has found that student teachers in such programs are generally more confident and more enthusiastic than their peers in traditional teacher education programs. Margaret aptly discusses what she calls "teacher-fantasies," or assumptions about what it means to be a teacher before one enters the field and develops as a practitioner. Teacher-fantasies, Margaret wisely realizes, are just that, and are essentially left behind once one moves forward into seeing the need for inquiry about one's teaching practice.

Alsup (2006) writes, "the most immediately and obviously 'successful' teacher education students (defined by those who took secondary teaching jobs after graduation) . . . were those who were given the opportunity and the necessary guidance to begin to see complex connections among their educational memories, their university education, their practical school and teaching experiences, and their personal or core ideologies" (p. 45). Margaret, throughout the second and third chronologies, is already able to make these connections. She speaks of the learning process she undertook during her time at Argentine Middle School and the time she needed to learn and listen and better understand the community and students.

THE FOURTH CHRONOLOGY: THE CUMULATIVE EXPERIENCE OF ONE'S ORIENTATION TOWARD SCHOOLING

Britzman (1991) describes how the fourth chronology begins with one's teaching career. At this point in time, Heidi and Margaret were still connected through social media. However, distance and time caused their worlds to not intersect in the same way as when Margaret was a preservice teacher. However, the event that Margaret describes below, pivotal in Margaret's teaching career, was one that Heidi noticed and followed on social media. Margaret's participation in a teacher and special service provider strike in spring 2019 is described next:

On an unseasonably warm January day, a close coworker and I walked into a church ready to cast our vote as union members in support of going on strike. As we walked, we reflected on our frustrations surrounding the situation. We shared opinions on the difficult decision we knew we needed to make, and we considered the possibility of state labor officials intervening.

Negotiations with our teacher union and the district concerning a "fair, transparent and professional salary plan" began much earlier, almost two years prior. I did not take an active interest in union involvement in those early discussions. Somewhere between assignments to grade, curriculum to curate, emails to draft, after-school clubs to supervise, along with the 2999 other tabs left open in my teacher brain, I found myself on the outskirts of the exact union partnership I hoped to uphold. It wasn't until the word "strike" was mentioned at a union meeting in the fall of 2018 when the reality of my engagement in my teacher union became palpable.

Each article I read and salary table I scrutinized sparked my interest and encouraged me to stand up and lean in. Without a clear idea of what to do or how to manage social activism while teaching ninety-plus seventh graders eight hours each day, I called upon my resilience and what my family does best: I started to talk. I became active in conversations with coworkers closest to me. The "dinner table" became hallways and classrooms. I connected regularly with union directors and listened to a multitude of perspectives from educators around the district.

I was nervous. I was eager. I was energized. I knew my actions were bolstered by the successful collective bargaining of labor unions before me. I knew that to serve the beautiful minds I teach, I needed to protect the sacred work of public education. However, I was naive in thinking this would be easy to do. My first encounter with a school colleague awakened me to the reality that the same people who extol the virtues of their own profession may disagree with the opportunity to advocate for it.

In one instance, a senior team lead asked me why I would disrupt the school routine so much without knowing for sure whether my activism would work. To her, I was just another starry-eyed millennial with an agenda. To her, the union was asking too much. This outlook was not uncommon in my school building. The people who once contemplated with me about how our dreams of being a teacher could thrive while also mastering the overwhelming pressures of public education suddenly disagreed with my perspective on how to save it.

Since my heart has always been deeply invested in my community, I knew I needed to continue engaging in thoughtful dialogue regardless of coworkers' disapproval. Though even with this confidence, the tears still came regularly. It took getting back up again and again to remember my truth. In hindsight, my first conversation about the strike was invaluable. It reminded me of the litany of excuses vilifying teachers for who they are and what they do. And more importantly, it gave me the courage I needed to continue discourse.

Conversations in the hallway changed to conversations at happy hour. Open doors became closed. I recognized it was not my job to get 100 percent of my school staff to think like me. I was no "sage" and I needed no platform to persuade opinion. I did, however, feel an urge to empower those around me to find their own answers. I felt passionate to lead and communicate the "good fight" for our students. I needed to remain awake. I needed to invite all perspectives to the table. I needed to remain vigilant and confront the challenge head-on.

After seven years in the classroom, it is clear to me that while the virtues of teachers are often recognized, our voices are not. The strike showed me otherwise.

I began day one of the teacher strike in sheer fright of the unknown. By day two my fear had transformed to pure empowerment! By day three, I was prepared to make it through another picket line in single-digit temperatures and I was ready for what was expected to be another marathon-long bargaining session.

To my surprise, community members greeted us at the front of school each day with a spread of coffee, hand warmers, and lots and lots of donuts. What struck me most was realizing that their compassion was more than just feeding cold, hungry, tired teachers. Their compassion to us meant their care for students and that meant people beyond our picket line were listening to our voices.

Yes, the essence of the strike was over how much and under what structure teachers and special service providers got paid. But at its heart I was fighting less for money and more for the respect for public education. We matter. Our students matter. It was time the district listened. We called upon our bravery and vowed to use our voice to speak up for what needed to change.

As one of five strike captains for my building, I was responsible for organizing a variety of moving parts before, during, and after the strike. But my favorite responsibility took me back to cheerleading on the sidelines. I carried a bullhorn and ran up and down the picket line leading the chants our fearless teachers shouted in unison. Because I needed my hands free, my picket sign hung around my neck. It read, "When we stand up for ourselves, we stand up for our students." I repeated this phrase in my head as a constant reminder that what I was doing during the strike was for students and teachers across the district, not just at my school.

At one point I paused to catch my breath and give my nearly frozen hands and feet reprieve. I watched 80 percent of our school staff passionately and relentlessly march in front of our school, well aware of the students inside without their teachers. As loudly as they chanted, as fiercely as they marched, I knew every single one of them, including myself, wanted more to be teaching. However, we acknowledge that we were not going to become inert with despair when things seemed wrong. Just as we teach our students, we accepted our responsibility, relied on our resilience, and self-advocated.

When the teacher strike reached its official end, it was Valentine's Day. Many of us were dressed in layers ready to picket for the fourth day. Just before dawn, I found myself scrambling for clarity as I listened to the tentative agreement made while on a conference call with our regional union representative. Joyous screams mixed with astonished tears. When I left bargaining at 8:00 p.m. the night before, the district and union still had many parts to sew up. Now, with the morning sky still dark, an actual agreement was being signed. I wanted to celebrate but there was still so much I didn't know, there was still so much I needed to do. I was certain of one thing. I would return to the classroom the next day and teach. I hoped we would be welcomed back to our school gracefully. Unfortunately, the reality was far different.

I believe most of us on strike recognized the importance of those who stayed in the building and continued to support students. In turn we hoped our colleagues would also understand why we made the difficult decision to go on strike. Yes, we wanted recognition of our historic win for education, but we wanted more to be welcomed back to our classroom routines, once again putting the development of our students first. My building's response was the exact opposite.

Our administration silenced our exuberance. We were told we did not put students first and embarrassed administration the day the tentative agreement was signed. When asked if we could walk into the building all together as a unified staff, we were told it was inappropriate and unnecessary. Some teachers who did not go on strike ignored those who did. We became the "strikers" and the strike became the "situation."

At first, I did what many of us do in uncomfortable situations. I tried to remember the big picture and the win we brought to our students, schools, and communities. I smiled off contempt from coworkers and told myself to be proud of my actions. I was one of three-quarters of teachers from around the district who helped reform an entire pay system that now provided stability for students and equitable pay for teachers. There was so much to be proud of, but nevertheless, I felt a burden to be quiet. And the message from administration at an all-staff meeting one week after returning to work left me feeling even more ignored.

Administration focused on how we as a staff needed to act and feel. The message centered on moving forward and we were told to "fake it 'til we make it." Grace for personal decisions was not given. Compassion for personal beliefs was left out. It felt like we were once again expected to be perfect machines.

Our experience during the strike was intensely emotional. Our common sentiment gave us a chance to get to know each other on an entirely different level. The strike opened opportunity to see each other as humans. We laughed. We cried. We empathized about fears and agreed about truths. We rallied together, listened together, waited in anticipation together, and regarded each other as courageous heroes who might have been afraid but who challenged the status quo regardless.

The strike was the best professional development I have ever had. Every conversation was personal. There was no blanket curriculum molding us into systemized thinkers. We were free to think and so became creatively united. We wanted a workplace that empowered us to learn, grow, and collaborate meaningfully. The reality was this was happening for free outside from school leaders and costly professional development sessions. We needed each other, so we provided unwavering support for each other. It was basic human nature at its finest. We did not know what the next hour, day, or week looked like, so we found optimism in "being together now." We knew the powerful influence we have with students daily and we were developing this power alongside each other on the picket lines.

Margaret's narrative ends with the statement, "the strike was the best professional development I have ever had." Margaret aligns her participation in the strike with a view of teacher professional development in which teachers are self-directed and active participants in their learning. Oftentimes, teacher professional development involves notions of working *on* teachers rather than *with* teachers (Loughran, 2017).

In such a model, teachers are not recognized for the knowledge they bring and are instead positioned as recipients of the knowledge of others. This belief underscores the idea that effective professional development will produce superior teachers (Supovitz, 2001), which will then translate into higher levels of student achievement. Yet professional development models that remain dominant and are so-called effective tend to argue for a focus on the technical and practical aspects of teaching (Darling-Hammond & Richardson, 2009).

While such models may have a place in teachers' learning, Margaret's assertions confirm that high-quality professional development may take other forms where teachers themselves, are the catalysts for their own learning. Studies (e.g., Smith, 2017) that validate this perspective of professional learning include those that assert that professional development for teachers must (1) foster self-efficacy, (2) align reason with action, and (3) value emerging expertise. Margaret's participation in the strike met all of the above goals of a vision of teacher professional development that places teachers' own agency and knowledge at the core.

THE FIFTH CHRONOLOGY: TRANSFORMATION

Now we expand on Britzman's (1991) four chronologies by adding a fifth chronology. The fifth chronology emphasizes the process of continual renewal that teachers must undertake in order to reinvigorate their practice. The fifth chronology is one of transformation, a theme that highlights moving forward in one's career and pushing oneself to develop new interests and competencies. In the following narrative, Margaret reflects on how her experience keeps pushing her forward.

Education is political. Because of the politics involved, people in education often take personal offense when encountering differences in opinion. Sadly, be it administration versus teachers or district versus school, the involved parties often seem to fear honest discourse because it may produce a negative emotional response. Take my administration's response to the looming end of the strike. Culture is set from the top down. The fact that my administration's actions sought more to demoralize than strengthen our value as educators created a heavy challenge for many teachers in my building who went on strike, especially myself.

While it is easy to interpret a challenge like this as paralyzing, for me, it did the opposite. The challenge made me want to speak out more. It opened my eyes to sensitiveness of humanity and how natural it is for some individuals to accuse another's actions as being wrong and dismiss their own behav-

ior as unavoidable. I realized that while tolerance is a tenet of education, one's need to protect one's ego may interfere with one's ability to practice it.

As uncomfortable and unfortunate as my return to work poststrike was, the experience taught me to approach different perspectives with humility and mindfulness. Multiple perspectives can coexist even if the individuals themselves are not unified. I now believe that understanding another's perspective does not mean dismantling my own. Reaching understanding means allowing time to share truths—and this starts with conversation.

As I move forward in my career as a classroom teacher, senior team leader of curriculum, and teacher coach, I must remain mindful of my own thoughts instead of immediately perceiving a statement, reaction, or belief as offensive. Even though this mindset may seem obvious to any professional, my experiences have shown me it is easy to overlook. Sometimes it takes an adverse situation to integrate new perspectives, people, and goals into your life and propel you forward in your career. Predictability and routine garner no challenge. For me, my desire to transform as a teacher is rooted in a firm belief to overcome each obstacle I encounter with resilience and self-efficacy. Some challenges may never be easily conquered, but they can become easier the more you engage.

We all know great teachers inspire students to be great. And over the course of my teaching career, I have learned that being great begins with my own inner drive for transformation. Am I fulfilled? Am I complacent? Will I back down from challenges or stand in the arena? How does an experience like this awaken the need to engage meaningfully in my profession? Remaining critically conscious of one's own development is the true measure of growth, both personally and professionally.

Margaret's statement, "understanding another's perspective does not mean dismantling my own," speaks to her embrace of a stance that is inclusive of multiple perspectives rather than binary perspectives that separate views into an us/them, or pro/con stance. Such binary conceptions are ingrained in our thinking and difficult to undo; it is Margaret's deep experience through participation in the strike that initiated her assertion that different views can coexist.

In university-based teacher education, Margaret's trajectory must be taken seriously. How can teacher educators know that they must urge beginning teachers to be not only pedagogically informed but also politically informed? How can teacher educators continue to foster beginning teachers' commitment to the profession as one premised on intellectual engagement, moral commitment, and political action? Margaret exemplifies this stance, and it is from such a place that teacher educators can gain ideological clarity.

The chronologies of teacher development, explored in this chapter, remind teachers and teacher educators that deep participation and commitment begets transformation. Without participation and commitment, it is impossible to change and adapt as time goes on. Yet at the same time that change and adaptation is stressed in the chronologies, the chronologies also point to the importance of the foundation on which change is built.

The foundation of one's biography and one's teacher education program and the student teaching experience are the precursors to ongoing change and transformation. In teacher education, it is important that change and challenge equip preservice teachers to desire ongoing transformation and growth. It is the quest for ongoing transformation—the kind that pushes teachers and teacher educators to grow, change, and continue to encounter new challenges—that is truly key to how teachers persist.

REFERENCES

Alsup, J. (2006). *Teacher identity discourses: Negotiating personal and professional discourses.* Mahwah, NJ: Lawrence Erlbaum.

Boyd, A. S. (2017). *Social justice literacies in the English classroom.* New York, NY: Teachers College Press.

Britzman, D. P. (1991). *Practice makes practice: A critical study of learning to teach.* Albany, NY: State University of New York Press.

Connor, K. R. & Killmer, N. (2001). Cohorts, collaboration, and community: Does contextual teacher education really work? *Action in Teacher Education, 23*(3), 46–53.

Darling-Hammond, L., & Richardson, N. (2009). Research review/teacher learning: What matters. *Educational Leadership, 66*(5), 46–53.

Loughran, J. (2017). Foreword. In K. Smith, *Teachers as self-directed learners: Active positioning through professional learning* (pp. v-vi). Gateway East, Singapore: Springer.

Sandholtz, J. H., & Wasserman, K. (2001). Student and cooperating teachers: Contrasting experiences in teacher preparation. *Action in Teacher Education, 23*(3), 54–65.

Smith, K. (2017). *Teachers as self-directed learners: Active positioning through professional learning.* Gateway East, Singapore: Springer.

Supovitz, J. A. (2001). Translating teaching practice into improved student achievement. *Yearbook National Society for the Study of Education, 2,* 81–98.

Yosso, T. (2006). *Critical race counterstories along the Chicana/Chicano educational pipeline.* New York, NY: Routledge.

Chapter Six

Beyond Reacting

One New Teacher's Reenvisioning of Top-Down Accountability Initiatives

Meghan A. Kessler and Arpan Patel

Top-down educational reform, especially that which is driven by neoliberalism, has become commonplace in many schools (Apple, 2001). These initiatives can result in restrictive curriculum, an overemphasis on testing, and deprofessionalization of teachers (Au, 2011; Ball, 2003; Zeichner, 2010). The manifestations of neoliberal ideologies are diverse and but the reliance on market logics such as competition and efficiency are widespread (Au & Ferrare, 2015). Such reforms are especially commonplace in urban settings that have been subjected to years of slim resource allocation and private-sector influences (Au, 2010).

In particular, many such reforms seek to leverage market logics for school improvement but lead to disempowered teachers and silenced community voices. More specifically, scholars have documented higher rates of teacher attrition in deregulated charter schools (Miron & Applegate, 2007; Renzulli et al., 2011; Rich, 2013), and greater autonomy for teachers but challenging work schedules (Ni, 2012). These findings are reason for concern for new teachers. Furthermore, charter schools have taken the place of many neighborhood schools, but their reliance on deregulation and competition has increased exclusionary discipline policies (Torres & Golann, 2018) and challenges for families of color with students who have dis/abilities (Waitoller & Super, 2017).

In order to investigate the impact of neoliberal reform and market logics on an individual teacher, this chapter explores the experiences of Arpan, a third-year social studies teacher, and his former preservice teacher educator,

Meghan. After sharing a bit of context, reflective narratives from Arpan's initial years teaching in urban high schools are paired with corresponding narratives from Meghan to provide a window into our efforts to make sense of larger contexts at play and the learning gleaned through this dialogue. In this way, learning has been a "two-way street" for the two of them and is an example of how relationships between teachers and teacher educators sustain agency in complex educational contexts.

The narratives are organized under the themes of tension and persistence. The first set of narratives follows the heading titled Tensions Created by Neoliberal Ideologies. In them, Arpan discusses personal and professional interaction with market logics in Chicago Public Schools, and Meghan reflects on her own learning through his experiences. The following section, Resisting and Reenvisioning for Professional Persistence, advances a second narrative set in which Arpan discusses his efforts to resist feelings of defeat and to reenvision his context for his own persistence and professional growth as Meghan responds. In this way, we reflexively move beyond simply *reacting* to this context to *enacting* agency in light of relatively rigid reform contexts (Ball et al., 2011). The chapter will close with conclusions and implications for teacher education and early career teacher learning or support.

TEACHER AND TEACHER EDUCATOR POSITIONALITY: ARPAN AND MEGHAN LEARN TOGETHER

Arpan is a teacher who identifies as a male of color and social studies educator in the Chicago public school district, facilitating learning for students at a neighborhood school on the west side of the city. Meghan is an assistant professor of teacher education at a public liberal arts university. She identifies as a white woman. Before pursuing her doctorate, she was a middle and high school social studies teacher. We met during the 2016–2017 academic year while Arpan was a student in Meghan's secondary social studies methods course at a large research institution where Meghan was completing her degree. Arpan is now a teacher in Chicago, Meghan is an assistant professor at a new university, and we continue to collaborate. Arpan's narratives are provided with brief contextualizing literature and details in order to situate his experience with market logics.

TENSIONS CREATED BY NEOLIBERAL IDEOLOGIES

During Arpan's student teaching semester and his first two years in the classroom, it quickly became evident to him that he had entered a context that was even more complex than he first appreciated. Furthermore, he began to realize that his experiences as a teacher candidate and new teacher echoed what he experienced as an elementary and secondary student. Growing up in the same large urban area where he would eventually teach provided Arpan with a certain depth of perspective on the experiences of teachers, students, and families in this community.

After moving to the "other side of the desk," Arpan reflected on his experience as a learner in Chicago. He realized that his family's decision to leave the city for a well-resourced suburban school district was situated within larger institutional, political, and social trends. Under the tenure of Arne Duncan as CEO, Chicago's public schools were caught in the confluence of high-stakes testing, decreased state funding, and rapid privatization (Brown et al., 2009), exacerbating the negative effects of the economic and racial segregation already present in the city. Yet, as mayoral and district leadership shifted, the closing of neighborhood schools and growth of charter schools continued. Likewise, the popularity of neoliberal reforms expanded in Chicago and nationally, with emphasis on school choice and competition (Au, 2009; Lipman, 2015).

In Chicago, Duncan's policies were a catalyst for the expansion of neoliberalism with the passage of the Renaissance 2010 (Ren2010) plan, which sought to close neighborhood schools and replace them with charter-based schools that could leverage market forces such as competition for reform (Lipman, 2011). By 2019, more than two hundred neighborhood schools had closed, most replaced by charter schools managed by private nonprofits. In some cases, school buildings were turned over and reopened under different management multiple times within a few years (Lutton et al., 2018).

The neighborhood schools that did stay open were labeled as "other" by school choice advocates and city politicians, inspiring increased "regula[tion] and penalizing mandates within school choice policies" (Bell, 2015, p. 141). While the influence of market logics progressed, Arpan left the city to attend a teacher preparation program, and eventually came back to the city for his student teaching and first job.

While he lived through some of these challenges as a student, the school where Arpan would eventually teach experienced intensive reform and accountability initiatives that resulted in a school culture steeped in neoliberal discourse. He experienced firsthand the integration of corporate methodologies relying on meritocratic tropes and the stress that the emphasis on high test scores, "grit" overall, and "no excuses" have on students of color (Au, 2016; Golann et al., 2019). These experiences influenced his personal and professional perspectives, creating tensions and opportunities for growth.

At the same time, Meghan stayed in contact with Arpan after graduation, often inquiring about his progress and the challenges and successes he faced in his first few years. Although it's a commonly held assumption that teachers may struggle early in their careers, it was clear that Arpan's experiences were uniquely complex and tied to market-oriented reform. However, Arpan maintained a distinct perspective toward his experience. We spoke periodically throughout the year, discussing the challenges he was facing. As Arpan helped Meghan learn about the realities of teachers beholden to neoliberal reform efforts, Meghan suggested things for Arpan to read that may contextualize his day to day.

The tension Arpan was experiencing at his school was largely attributed to the network's assumption that market forces like competition were the best tools for improving the quality of education for the city's historically marginalized populations. While almost blatantly explicit in Arpan's context, this trend is nothing new nor is it unique to Chicago. As Ball (2004) asserts, competitiveness and the production of "quality" measurable products are the hallmarks of a system that has reified education as primarily serving economic ends.

The by-product, unfortunately, is the quantification and surveillance of individual subjects (i.e., teachers). They were caught in the middle of a Foucauldian "epistemic shift—that is a profound change in the underlying set of rules governing the production of discourses, the conditions of knowledge" (Ball 2004, p. 24) and the overall definition of "good" teacher or school. Fortunately, Arpan was able to cultivate agency in his school, seeking out opportunities to enact the collegiality and justice-oriented perspective he so valued. This began as a strategy necessary for learning and survival that grew into a way to reenvision his professional relationships as a form of resistance to the competitiveness enforced by network leadership. The narratives describing these tensions follow.

Narrative 1

Arpan was born and raised in Chicago. For its many denizens the city has long resembled a fractal of American opportunity. On the premise of hope and ambition, countless immigrants come to this city, seeking a fruitful life in another part of the world. On the premise of hope and ambition, prior to his birth, Arpan's parents left their native country and settled in Chicago as immigrants looking to build a fruitful life for their future children. As time passed, like countless other families, Arpan's mother and father realized these dreams yet saw them challenged when it came time to enroll their children in school.

Although public schooling is a declared right for all children in the United States, in Chicago, Arpan's family faced competing notions of educational opportunity. While he was growing up, his neighborhood school was inadequately resourced and neglected, while the city's high-quality institutions tiered enrollment based on test scores, location, or socioeconomic standing. This prompted his family to leave the city for the suburbs in pursuit of more equitable education. The well-resourced suburban schools Arpan attended in his later elementary and secondary years afforded him the opportunity to attend a well-respected state university and pursue a career in education. His experiences left him appreciative yet frustrated with the lack of equity he witnessed.

Narrative 2

As when Arpan was a young student, his journey as a teacher in the city provided similar insight into the business ethos that governs much of the district's educational policy. Early on, serving a professional role at one of Chicago's largest charter networks, he observed school leaders and administrators operating under a corporate methodology that often ran counter to the best interests of students, teachers, and communities.

For example, the diverse learner population (or students with specific learning needs) were effectively weeded out through disciplinary action or academic probation, leaving the school mainly to serve top performers. For the students who stayed, the mantra was to adapt and overcome, letting go of all excuses that may stand in the way of success. This all-or-nothing approach to success took its toll on students. For example, at one report-card pickup, a student in her senior year had an emotional breakdown because she was not eligible to enroll at a major university or pursue an alternative career path right after high school.

In that moment, Arpan clearly was not feeling able to "persevere and overcome," despite repeatedly being told so for four straight years. The charter network strictly defined success as being college and career ready, defining students' worth through the metrics of productivity, rather than appreciating these young adolescents' broader humanity. Similarly, teachers were appraised and bartered in relation to narrow measures of results and output.

In the charter network, teachers were expected to work long hours with few breaks in their schedules, all while receiving less compensation in comparison to other educators in the city. Many of Arpan's colleagues were uncertified workers or first-year educators looking for an entryway into teaching, enabling administrators to exploit a marginalized labor force for maximum gain. In this condition, some teachers would jettison professional solidarity by acting against the interests of their coworkers in hopes of advancing through the ranks.

One teacher at the school, for instance, would sit in on meetings related to unionization, only to report all happenings directly back to the principal. At its core, the network promoted the idea that teachers existed as individuals in competition for status, while clouding collective power and balance. At staff meetings, teachers who served the interests of the network in place of their fellows spoke in similar terms: "I do not have the same problems in my classroom. . . . I do not understand why we are complaining. . . . I find there is help if someone is just willing to ask."

For teachers and students alike, the goal was to persevere and overcome with no excuses, absent of context or limitation. Arpan's charter school purported a race to achievement for all poor and working people in education, a competition supposedly unhindered by the bounds of other social frameworks. At the start of each year, new teachers would simply take the place of the many who left, and newly enrolled students would soon find themselves seeking an education at another school. As with all competitions, the outcome was isolated achievement—full of few winners and many losers.

Narrative 3

Among the many things Meghan learned from talking with Arpan about his perspectives on his first few years in this school reform context was the "real-life" impact on teachers and their professional relationships. It was concerning to learn that the gaze of network leadership permeated every aspect of these teachers' work, including their relationships with each other. While Meghan was worried about Arpan's job satisfaction and ability to persist in this setting, she learned an important lesson about the true power of a theoretical base in teacher preparation.

Although Arpan was a bit more widely read than some of his preparation program peers, his curiosity about school policy and urban school reform helped put an inquisitive spin on his experience and their conversations. As is evidenced in the narratives above, he was able to step back and analyze the trends that were taking place in his school as part of a larger political and ideological trend in education.

For instance, his reading of Naomi Klein's (2007) reporting of the turnover of New Orleans's public school system to charter networks provided a lens through which to consider the narratives being presented by his own network leaders. These conversations with Arpan helped Meghan realize how much she would have benefited from the same in her first few years of teaching; it wasn't until graduate school that she was afforded the opportunity to name and analyze the sociopolitical forces at work our educational systems.

RESISTING AND REENVISIONING RELATIONSHIPS FOR PROFESSIONAL PERSISTENCE

As his career has progressed, Arpan found multiple outlets to manifest his desire for community-oriented schools. The most powerful of these is the solidarity he found in union membership and relationships with his colleagues. Arpan resisted the more troublesome manifestations of market logics in his school by reenvisioning his relationships with other teachers. The importance of collegial solidarity goes beyond simply being supportive of one another. Teachers and teacher educators alike can contribute to persistence in the field and the overall strength of the profession by nurturing relationships with each other. This can also contribute to reducing the research-practice gap that can unfortunately inhibit communication and collaborations between K–12 teachers and their university counterparts.

On a more personal level, Arpan found strength in being able to mentor a new colleague who joined the staff during his second year. Mentorship and collegiality became central to his mission and identity, and he relished the opportunity to help this younger colleague thrive. This experience was an informal enactment of the kind of mentoring that research has cited to be an important element in teacher retention (Smith & Ingersoll, 2004). While not an explicit prompt from Meghan, her experience with teacher induction and mentoring programs helped drive conversation with Arpan and generate new ideas in her own work.

As Meghan listened to Arpan's retelling of these stories, she was in the midst of working on a professional development research project in early career teacher mentoring and induction. This project intended to provide support for rural teacher-mentors who needed resources for their induction programs. Furthermore, the state of Illinois was experiencing a teacher shortage that began to energize conversations about teacher pay, job satisfaction, retention, and professional supports. Thanks to her conversations with Arpan, Meghan realized that the teachers participating in the project were also lacking opportunities for collegial conversations about their mentoring work due to their relatively isolated geographic locations. Therefore, she added an additional research question related to the affordances of cross-district professional networking, inspired by what she was learning from Arpan. Our narratives, which follow, describe how our persistence stems from resisting and reenvisioning relationships.

Narrative 1

At a recent professional development conference, a fellow teacher of Arpan's made the following joke in passing: "All of us got into this job thinking we would be some radicals in the classroom . . . only to see a piece of that spirit die more and more as each year passes." Although the remark was made with a comedic undertone, the essence the statement is one Arpan came to seriously reflect upon.

In becoming a teacher, Arpan was motivated by educational justice— providing access to schooling on equal terms—yet the systematic injustices were too much for one person to overcome. However, he found the communal power of teachers to be an effective response to a system that categorizes people as widgets, and began telling Meghan about these relationships.

For example, in his charter network, teachers had collectively worked to unionize, against the wishes of administration. While the battle for unionization was slightly contentious, it reminded Arpan of the importance of teachers' collective voice. He was able to establish a rapport with his colleagues while they discussed the importance of resisting the network's competitive tendencies, and felt less isolated than he had previously.

The following year, Arpan found a new role as a teacher in the Chicago Public School District. In spite of his new position at a non-charter school, the charter network had remained in his focus; charter teachers were seeking to form a coalition. Thus, union meetings at his new school included discussions on whether this outside faction should be admitted as members. Apprehension was strong as members of the Chicago Teacher's Union worried about leveraging resources to many uncertified professionals at these charter schools.

Despite these worries, members of the union echoed the sentiment that charter school teachers were engaged in the same line of public service as all other teachers and subject to the same forces that threatened all educators. By working together, teachers were stronger and ready to fight on behalf of educational justice in Chicago. Consequently, the coalition was authorized with a majority vote. The consolidation of power in effect enabled many of these charter teachers across the city to demand better working conditions for staff, humane treatment of students, and further checks and balances on authority.

Through the collective solidarity of our union, many of the city's communities stood in the face of Chicago's marketized system of education that was often otherwise unchallenged in policy and practice. Many charter schools are changing pay rates for staff, uniform policies for students, and being forced to respond to many other inquiries that were simply ignored years prior to the movement.

At the heart, solidarity matters in public education. At Arpan's school, teachers often point to one mantra: "Do not talk shit about other teachers." The saying is in place to encourage the trust needed to fight and enact agency for the greater good of students and educational justice. He and his colleagues are facing some of the more challenging teaching contexts, but there's comfort in knowing that they can all whisper to each other, "I have no idea what I'm doing" and seek support from colleagues. This vulnerability fosters trust among what would otherwise be an overwhelmed teaching staff.

Narrative 2

At the time Arpan was sharing his new learning about teacher unionization and collegiality, Meghan was engaged in the dissertation phase of her PhD program. She found the conversations with Arpan about collectivism and solidarity among teachers a generative concept for her analysis and teaching. For instance, she was working with data about teacher candidates' perceptions of teacher evaluation and licensure requirements. Arpan's critical reframing of the charter school competition and the destruction of neighborhood schools informed interview questions with her dissertation participants in which she sought to unpack their understanding of the political context of such measures.

Narrative 3

This past school year a new teacher had joined the staff at Arpan's school. Predictably, the new teacher faced the trials and tribulations of a person in the first year—classroom management issues, exhaustion, and the overall feeling of embarrassment in a public setting. Furthermore, these issues are of particular consequence at school, which is under an intense regulatory gaze. One day after school, Arpan approached this colleague and gave him a few words of advice that perhaps would have helped him early on in his career.

Simply, his colleagues paid no mind to the "quality" of his teaching; they valued the work he did for their school by taking on such a tough job in the first place and trying to do it again the next day. Moreover, his performance would not make or break the lives of however many children he taught. After all, Arpan had had a poor history teacher at one point, but had many other great ones to educate him later in life.

It takes a village to raise a child. If one teacher may make or break the life of a student, it may be a larger sign that the overall system of education in that young person's world is not sound. Schools and communities enhance the lives of children. Collectively teachers work together in building a fair, just, and equitable society. Individually, teachers stand against the overwhelming power of the educational marketplace in American schooling. With the trust of colleagues, teachers have the voice to advocate for what is true and enabling in the missional calling of the job. Despite the burdens they face, teachers are stronger together.

THE POWER OF COLLEGIALITY

These narratives bring to light the complexity of new teacher development at the intersection of school reform and market logics. They also highlight the opportunities present when teacher educators and their candidates collaborate. The following questions are raised by the above narratives. For practicing teachers or teacher candidates: How else have you seen market logics manifested at your school? How have you and your colleagues responded? For teacher educators: How are you challenging or reinforcing these ideologies in your work with students? What useful counterbalances have you found to the negative impacts of these ideologies?

Arpan found strength in his collegial relationships and community, and Meghan found inspiration as a researcher and teacher educator, each demonstrating the sustaining power of cross-contextual and long-term relationships. Just as Arpan found strength in his community of educators, Meghan grew from her conversations with her former student. There are implications for teacher educators and teachers to consider after reading these narratives. First, teacher educators should consider the extent to which they are equipping teacher candidates and teachers to fill their theoretical toolbox. Arpan's ability to persist and reenvision a challenging school context was supported, in part, by his engagement with critical theorists and policy commentators. Therefore, one way to counter the reductive capacities of market logics in school reform is to enable the consideration of complexities through theoretical or political lenses.

While there is great value in the practical and technical elements of teacher preparation and continuing education, these should not be done to the exclusion of deep critical thinking. Second, these narratives also highlight the sustaining power of collegiality across the career spectrum. Our conversations provided Arpan with the chance to talk through some of the challenges he was experiencing in his first few years of teaching, and likewise, Meghan (a new teacher educator herself), was able to generate new lines of inquiry and ideas for her methods and seminar courses, as stated above. The cyclical benefits of this teacher–teacher educator relationship are certainly among millions, but should not be taken for granted.

Finally, this chapter may be used as a springboard for conversations among teachers and teacher educators who may be subject to similar accountability or reform movements. Research has found that reform contexts and the discourses tied to those efforts are significant forces in the formation of teacher identity (e.g., Buchanan, 2015). Even when the sociocultural influences on a teacher's identity create tension, new opportunities for agency are also forged in the resistance against or the negotiation of oppositional or challenging elements (Ruohotie-Lyhty, 2018). As Meghan learned from Arpan, the discourses of power and accountability may be strong—even overwhelming—but they are also opportunities for professional learning and collegiality.

REFERENCES

Apple, M. W. (2001). *Educating the "right" way: Markets, standards, God, and inequality.* New York, NY: Routledge.

Au, W. (2009). Obama, where art thou? Hoping for change in US education policy. *Harvard Educational Review, 79*(2), 309–320.

Au, W. (2010). *Unequal by design: High-stakes testing and the standardization of inequality.* New York, NY: Routledge.

Au, W. (2011). Teaching under the new Taylorism: High-stakes testing and the standardization of the 21st century curriculum. *Journal of Curriculum Studies, 43*(1), 25–45.

Au, W. (2016). Meritocracy 2.0: High-stakes, standardized testing as a racial project of neoliberal multiculturalism. *Educational Policy, 30*(1), 39–62.

Au, W., & Ferrare, J. J. (Eds.). (2015). *Mapping corporate education reform: Power and policy networks in the neoliberal state.* New York, NY: Routledge.

Ball, S. J. (2003). The teacher's soul and the terrors of performativity. *Journal of Education Policy, 18*(2), 215–228.

Ball, S. J. (2004, June 17). *Education for sale! The commodification of everything?* Lecture presented at the University of London for the 2004 King's Annual Education Lecture 2004, London, UK.

Ball, S. J., Maguire, M., & Braun, A. (2011). *How schools do policy: Policy enactments in secondary schools.* London: Routledge.

Bell, S. (2015). Mapping the discourse of neoliberal education reform: Space, power, and access in Chicago's Renaissance 2010 debate. In W. Au & J. J. Ferrare (Eds.), *Mapping corporate education reform: Power and policy networks in the neoliberal state* (pp. 126–146). New York, NY: Routledge.

Brown, J., Gutstein, E., & Lipman, P. (2009). Arne Duncan and the Chicago success story: Myth or reality? *Rethinking Schools, 23*(3), 10–14.

Buchanan, R. (2015). Teacher identity and agency in an era of accountability. *Teachers and Teaching, 21*(6), 700–719.

Golann, J. W., Debs, M., & Weiss, A. L. (2019). "To be strict on your own": Black and Latinx parents evaluate discipline in urban choice schools. *American Educational Research Journal,* 1–32. doi: 10.3102/0002831219831972

Klein, N. (2007). *The shock doctrine: The rise of disaster capitalism.* New York, NY: Macmillan.

Lipman, P. (2011). *The new political economy of urban education: Neoliberalism, race, and the right to the city.* New York, NY: Routledge.

Lipman, P. (2015). Urban education policy under Obama. *Journal of Urban Affairs, 37*(1), 57–61.

Lutton, L., Vevea, B., Karp, S., Cardona-Maguigad, A., & McGee, K. (2018, December 3). A generation of school closings. WBEZ 91.5 Chicago. Retrieved from https://interactive.wbez.org/generation-school-closings/

Miron, G., & Applegate, B. (2007). *Teacher attrition in charter schools.* Tempe, AZ: Education Policy Research Unit and Boulder, CO: Education and the Public Interest Center. Retrieved June 27, 2019 from https://nepc.colorado.edu/publication/teacher-attrition-charter-schools

Ni, Y. (2012). Teacher working conditions in charter schools and traditional public schools: A comparative study. *Teachers College Record (114),* 030303. Retrieved July 2, 2019 from http://www.tcrecord.org/Content.asp?ContentId=16301

Renzulli, L. A., Parrott, H. M., & Beattie, I. R. (2011). Racial mismatch and school type: Teacher satisfaction and retention in charter and traditional public schools. *Sociology of Education, 84*(1), 23–48. http://dx.doi.org/10.1177/0038040710392720

Rich, M. (2013, August 26). At charter schools, short careers by choice. *New York Times.* Retrieved from www.nytimes.com/2013/08/27/education/at-charter-schools-short-careers-by-choice.html

Ruohotie-Lyhty, M. (2018). Teacher identity and political construction. In P. Schutz, J. Hong, & D. Cross Francis (Eds.), *Research on teacher identity* (pp. 25–36). Cham, Switzerland: Springer.

Smith, T. M., & Ingersoll, R. M. (2004). What are the effects of induction and mentoring on beginning teacher turnover? *American Educational Research Journal, 41*(3), 681–714.

Torres, A. C., & Golann, J. W. (2018). NEPC Review: "Charter Schools and the Achievement Gap." Boulder, CO: National Education Policy Center. Retrieved from http://nepc.colorado.edu/thinktank/review-no-excuses

Waitoller, F. R., & Super, G. (2017). School choice or the politics of desperation? Black and Latinx parents of students with dis/abilities selecting charter schools in Chicago. *Education Policy Analysis Archives, 25*(55). http://dx.doi.org/10.14507/epaa.25.2636

Zeichner, K. (2010). Competition, economic rationalization, increased surveillance, and attacks on diversity: Neo-liberalism and the transformation of teacher education in the U.S. *Teaching and Teacher Education, 26*(8), 1544–1552. doi: 10.1016/j.tate.2010.06.004

Chapter Seven

Growing to Thrive

The Story of Two Colleagues Prospering in an Era of Standards-Based Education

Eric D. Moffa and Toni M. Poling

This chapter examines the ways two former high school colleagues, an English teacher and a social studies teacher, thrived in a standards-based educational environment by seeking pathways for professional development and personal growth. These pathways led each colleague toward innovative pedagogies in our respective disciplines and also prompted each to take on roles as teacher leaders. Ultimately, our emphasis on professional growth resulted in one teacher being named the 2017 West Virginia Teacher of the Year and the other becoming a teacher educator.

In response to her students' needs, Toni, the award-winning English teacher, developed authentic reading and nonformulaic writing experiences for her students. Toni breathed "place" into English language arts (ELA) standards, which are sometimes criticized as placeless (see Gruenewald, 2003, p. 8), by creating a unit on the opioid crisis in West Virginia that culminated in a student-drafted action plan. Similarly, Toni developed a unit that empowered students to tell their unique Appalachian stories by drafting a geographical autobiography, recording it, and producing a public podcast.

In Toni's state, teachers who were feeling the pressures of increasingly hostile policies and practices toward public education recently organized two teacher strikes to advocate for their students, schools, and state. The two strikes were successful in raising awareness to the needs of public education. Toni continues to be an agent of change, advocating for a shift to a more student-centered curriculum in her school, district, and state.

Eric, the former social studies teacher and current professor of education, reacted to a standards-based environment by recentering his instruction around aims for democratic citizenship and incorporating inquiry-based pedagogies. Capitalizing on the social and often latent political diversity of his students, Eric created a new elective course on discussing controversial political issues to foster students' skills and dispositions for civil deliberation and challenging myths of rural sameness.

Often thought to be cut from one political cloth, Appalachian students in Eric's class verbalized their normally dormant political opinions, revealing the diversity of thought that existed in one homogeneous-appearing group of students. Similarly, Eric infused values clarification and evidence interrogation into inquiry-based approaches to teaching history and government. These approaches elicited differences of opinions in his students and encouraged the evaluation of multiple perspectives that moved student learning from memorization to decision making.

In response to state and district emphases on covering standards and preparing for high-stakes tests, we modified our instruction to meet students' needs and prepare them more broadly for meaningful living. We leaned on our professional relationships, including our own as emerging teacher-leaders, for inspiration and strength to develop new pedagogies. Our model of growth helped us thrive despite external restraints, becoming better teachers and propelling our careers to new heights.

THE POLITICAL LANDSCAPE

We began our teaching careers in the early 2000s as the implementation of No Child Left Behind (NCLB) (2002) began to transform education. NLCB was an omnibus federal act that required states to develop curriculum standards, high-stakes testing, and accountability measures that included harsh consequences for underperforming schools. We taught in a small town in West Virginia. Our state school system adopted content standards and objectives (CSOs) for the core content areas, which were tested by an end-of-year statewide exam.

The results of the state exam were used to compare a school's performance against other schools in the county and state. Districts whose schools failed to meet Adequate Yearly Progress (AYP) faced a state takeover (Associated Press, 2009). Our district implemented a curriculum mapping tool that required teachers to map their classroom instruction to the CSOs. Also, the district implemented benchmark assessments (aka practice tests) throughout the academic year in preparation for the end-of-year exams, ultimately leading to a loss of instructional time for students as teachers were obligated to implement the required assessments and report scores back to district administrators.

The effects of high-stakes testing have been well examined in educational literature (Au, 2007; Berryhill et al., 2009; Cavanagh, 2012; Moe, 2003). Moe (2003) frames NCLB and its associated state-level curriculum mandates as an external control of classroom teachers that mirrors other bureaucratic organizations in a top-down approach to influence workers' behaviors. These types of policy-mandated education accountability measures are associated with teachers' emotional exhaustion, particularly through their lack of self-efficacy and time to address the numerous standards (Berryhill et al., 2009). One survey of teachers found that high-stakes testing increases teacher burnout and drives good teachers out of the profession (Cavanagh, 2012). In addition to its effect on teachers' emotional well-being, high-stakes testing often strips relevancy from curricula and scales back student-centered activities (Au, 2007).

Au (2007) demonstrated via a metasynthesis of forty-nine studies on high-stakes testing that the primary effect of high-stakes testing was a narrowing of curriculum content and an increase in teacher-centered instruction. Others critique standards-based approaches to schooling through a theoretical lens (Evans, 2001; Gruenewald, 2003; Vinson, 1999). Gruenewald (2003) cautions that a standardized curriculum is "placeless"; it does little to foster students' empathy or allow for the exploration of local places (p.8). Similarly, Vinson (1999) suggests that standards run contrary to democratic education and the localized nature of schooling.

In a minority of cases, standardized testing was shown to be a stimulus for curricular expansion, integration, and critical thinking. For example, Au (2007) reported on social studies teachers who incorporated critical literacy into their instruction. Grissom and colleagues (2014) compared a large data set of teacher surveys before and after NCLB and found that, despite media portrayals and popular anecdotes, NCLB did not adversely impact teachers' job satisfaction or commitment to their work and, in some cases, led to positive feelings of classroom control and administrative support.

These findings, however, should be moderated by the understanding that teachers' emotional exhaustion and burnout is not necessarily equivalent to their job satisfaction or commitment to the profession. These conditions may coexist, be held in tension, or fluctuate over time as curricular adaptations and district policies are formed in response to and negotiation with local needs. Similarly, some teachers, such as Toni and Eric, responded to NCLB by finding avenues for collaboration, autonomy, and professional growth.

NCLB's impact and legacy is complex; yet little doubt exists that it directed state-, district-, and school-level policies in the early twenty-first century. NCLB's top-down approach created additional pressures for teachers. Not only were teachers concerned with acting in the best interest of their students, but they also had the added pressure of meeting AYP targets; the standardization of their curriculum, instruction, and assessment; and the watchful eye of district and state political and educational leaders.

Ultimately, teachers were in classrooms across the United States making culturally relevant decisions daily that impacted their students' learning. The residual effects of legislation like NCLB led to a wave of teacher strikes and walkouts in recent years as teachers elevated their voices in advocacy for their students and schools. The question arises: what experiences enabled teachers to learn to thrive under the challenges of a standardized education environment? In light of calls for research on teacher identity to focus more on relationships and contexts (Beijaard et al., 2004), the remainder of this chapter conveys the experiences, reactions, and decisions that helped us bring meaningful, place-conscious activities to the forefront of our instruction in the face of a standards-based era.

FORGING PROFESSIONAL RELATIONSHIPS AND BECOMING TEACHER-LEADERS

New teachers report feeling isolated in their work and feeling pressures to be seen as an expert and independent educator from day one; yet Kardos and Johnson (2007) suggest these overwhelming feelings can be combated by forming schools with "integrated professional cultures, which promote frequent and reciprocal interaction among faculty members across experience levels" (p. 2083). As new teachers, we found ourselves on a staff of a school where nearly every colleague was older and more experienced.

While professional isolation loomed, we soon located experienced mentors in our departments and administration. Simultaneously, we were asked to teach Advanced Placement (AP) level courses in our respective disciplines and were asked to take on additional responsibilities through the school. While physically far from each other on the school campus in our first few years of teaching, we quickly realized a mirrored quality of dedication to the school and the profession in one another. Our professional relationship, mutual admiration, and dedication to the school positioned us to become leaders in our school, even in our early careers.

The district and school provided several avenues for beginning teachers to thrive. This included discipline-based professional learning communities (PLCs), which were monthly meetings with departmental colleagues to discuss innovative pedagogies and make action plans for implementation. Teachers were rewarded with continuous education credits from the district for their participation in PLCs. Similarly, our school collaborated with local universities as a professional development school (PDS), which provided opportunities for teachers to learn from university faculty and establish multiyear relationships with preservice teachers. Lastly, the district offered a mentoring program for National Board Certification (a status Toni achieved in 2013).

We both found professional networks beyond the walls of our school. This included attending yearly statewide institutes for AP in our content areas. AP institutes provided time and space for teachers from around the state to converge for a week of focused learning on pedagogy that emphasized learners rather than standards, a mindset shift for teachers who came into the classroom under the shadow of NCLB.

Back at our school, we took on leadership roles that, in part, hoped to inspire and improve the experiences of all staff. Eric served as faculty senate president, a position that Toni then filled when Eric moved into higher education. Toni served as the coordinator for student teachers, *High Schools That Work*, and eventually served as chair of the English department. Eric led an instructional practices inventory team (see Valentine, 2007). We both served on numerous hiring committees and were frequently tapped to assist with the development of school-wide improvement plans.

In our final three years as colleagues, Eric's classroom was moved to the same floor as Toni's classroom. We began to eat lunch together and discuss each other's curriculum; we shared many of the same AP students. The natural pairing of our content areas allowed us to talk through curricular decisions and work with our departments to move beyond the district-mandated curriculum guide to instructional activities designed to meet the most pressing needs of the students in our classrooms. Correspondingly, these informal conversations etched a tighter niche for us as teacher leaders as the school underwent major staff changes due to administration changes and teacher retirements. We both transitioned into mentoring roles for new hires in our departments—roles that enabled us to reconstruct our departments' cultures in fruitful ways. The following two sections highlight some of our student-centered curricular and pedagogical approaches.

CREATING READERS, WRITERS, AND THINKERS IN THE ENGLISH LANGUAGE ARTS CLASSROOM

The basics of literacy instruction are simple: students need to learn to read, write, listen, view, speak, and visually represent ideas (National Council of Teachers of English & International Reading Association, 1996). Embedded in that instruction, however, is the knowledge that today's world needs critical thinkers who recognize that there are multiple answers to every question and that decisions must be weighed, measured, and supported with evidence (Beers & Probst, 2017). Unfortunately, as Toni entered the teaching profession on the heels of NCLB, she entered an English classroom where recreational reading was seen as "soft" and critical thinking was often replaced by an expectation of surface-level thinking (Gallagher, 2015).

In her first teaching job in 2004, Toni was handed a teacher's edition of the student textbook, a printout of the state's CSOs (the state did not adopt the Common Core State Standards until 2011) for ELA, and little else. To her, the message was clear: use the book to teach to the end-of-year test so students could "pass" the state assessment, an exam devised to assess student knowledge in the core areas where all accountability was placed on the teacher, school, and district rather than the student.

Toni spent the next 180 days trying to do just that by focusing on multiple-choice assessments and plot construction in texts lacking cultural relevancy and place-consciousness for her students. Toni felt she was expected to teach what was in the textbook, a text already in the fifth year of its seven-year adoption cycle and one of the few choices approved by the State Department of Education for alignment to the state's content standards and year-end assessment. With AYP at stake, Toni felt the pressure to conform to the standardization of ELA instruction.

Having come from a strong teacher preparation program, Toni knew the pedagogy she was engaging was far from student-centered or best practice, but the district pressure to perform for the state assessment was a powerful motivator for a new teacher. As Toni began to seek out professional development to inform her professional practice, she was reminded of the importance of meeting the needs of learners in her classroom. She began to morph her personal pedagogy into instruction that works to disrupt the literary canon and provide place-conscious learning experiences for students.

TONI'S PERSONAL NARRATIVE

I spent the formative years of my career as an English teacher believing my purpose was to teach students to read and understand the literary canon, interspersed with a few of my personal favorites. When students would inevitably ask why I felt the need to force them through one challenging text or another I would often provide some glib response and move on to the next item on my carefully designed lesson plan. What I couldn't say to my students was that I didn't know why I was forcing them to read a particular text other than it was in my textbook and on my curriculum map; therefore it must be read. My lessons in those early years centered on understanding plot elements and character development. I was working so hard at researching and dissecting the texts that my students hardly had to work at all!

I was incredibly fortunate to be able to work with empowering colleagues (like Eric) who challenged my thinking about education and curriculum; colleagues who encouraged me to seek every opportunity for professional growth and professional development; colleagues who steered me toward some of my pedagogical heroes and embraced my desire to improve my own professional practice. My transformation into a thriving classroom teacher was truly realized, however, when I completed my National Board Certification, a process that required a level of professional self-reflection that irrevocably altered my understanding of pedagogy and curriculum.

Teaching in any state has its challenges, but teaching in a state whose teachers and schools have been under intense scrutiny, a state where our young people talk almost exclusively about leaving, a state in the midst of an opioid crisis, has provided me with a sense of clarity and purpose in the classroom (see Poling, 2018, to read about the teacher movement in my state). My students no longer suffer through pieces from the literary canon just because. My students complete geographic autobiographies that explore the power of place and our connection to the ground that holds our roots. These geographic autobiographies are recorded and released as podcasts so others can feel the connection to the mountains and the rivers we live amongst.

My students study the cause and effect of the opioid epidemic sweeping our state and the states that surround us, creating their own works of literature from the words of those in the midst of the battle. Their public service announcements on the crisis and its effects on their community and state brings a humanity to the epidemic often not portrayed in news coverage. My students are encouraged to take responsibility for their learning; to make connections with, and meaning from, the pieces we study; to challenge their own thinking on any given topic. My students constantly ask questions, but they no longer have to ask why we study a certain piece.

The past few years have shown the greatest growth in my professional practice. My teaching has morphed into a student-centered curriculum where learning is personal, important, and valued and I model vulnerability and transparency in decision making. My goal for my students is simple: I want them to leave my classroom better readers, writers, and thinkers than they entered it.

Still teaching ELA in a public school classroom, Toni continues to seek opportunities for professional development, although now she is often found *leading* sessions on learner-centered pedagogy and curricula. As a teacher-leader, Toni actively strives to elevate the teaching profession and to provide resources and support for new and struggling teachers that focus on the student and go beyond a textbook and a set of standards.

EMBRACING CONTROVERSIES IN THE SOCIAL STUDIES CURRICULUM

While the social studies content area has long been associated with preparing students for civic competency, little agreement exists about the best curriculum and methods to do such a task (Evans, 2004). Some forms of civics emphasize traditional citizenship roles, such as informed voting, obeying laws, and volunteering. Other progressive conceptions of civics emphasize group deliberations and community organizing, while still others highlight taking action to combat social injustice (Westheimer & Kahne, 2004).

Despite these competing aims, surveys demonstrate that teachers often emphasize the memorization of historic or governmental facts in social studies classes (CIRCLE, 2014; Torney-Purta, 2002)—an activity that aligns with content standards that innumerate such information. Yet democratic scholars critique such knowledge-based curriculum as inadequate to bring about a robust, participatory democracy (Westheimer & Kahne, 2004; Vinson, 1999). A curriculum centered on memorization of facts does little to prepare students for moral-laden decisions that are central to a democracy (Westheimer & Kahne, 2004).

Eric's early years as a teacher were dominated by a "sage on a stage" conception of teaching; a conception bolstered by state standards that had to be covered before the end-of-year exam. The school administration required standards be listed on every lesson plan and tracked on a monthly curriculum map to ensure they were addressed. State social studies standards mandated that students be able to identify and explain discipline-specific terms and concepts or use these concepts in higher-order thinking tasks like evaluation or analysis.

For example, students in the twelfth grade were asked, among other things, to outline the provisions of the PATRIOT Act and design a timeline of the civil rights movement. The standards were numerous and designated specific concepts, facts, and skills. The state adopted the Common Core Standards for English and math, but did not emphasize the literacy skills focused upon in the Common Core History/Social Studies standards, a subsection of English Language Arts Standards (Common Core State Standards Initiative, 2019).

Through in-service professional development and graduate studies at a local university, Eric restructured his courses and curricular aims, occasionally subverting the state-mandated standards to implement authentic, meaningful democratic experiences for his students that were not outlined in the state standards.

ERIC'S PERSONAL NARRATIVE

I used to believe that good teaching came naturally to me. I loved talking about the subject matter; I had a booming voice and a large stature that commanded students' attention; and I enjoyed talking with and mentoring teenagers. Yet daily I witnessed students suffering through my lectures with expressions of boredom and despondency. I knew of better models of instruction but found myself resorting back to lectures to cover the state-mandated content.

I soon forged relationships with teachers (like Toni) who set a high bar for the profession. I attended quality professional development. I learned about inquiry-based pedagogies in my disciplines from graduate courses. I came to realize that effective teaching requires much more than a booming voice. It requires specialized knowledge, skills, and a reflective disposition.

I began to adapt new pedagogies into my instruction. The history classes that I once dominated with lectures that covered state standards, where students struggled to stay awake, were transformed into history labs with students discussing competing interpretations of primary sources (see Lesh, 2011). Government classes that once emphasized rote memorization of facts became hotbeds of policy deliberations with students taking stances on controversial issues and evaluating different types of evidence (see Hess, 2009). My students began to share epiphanies that the seemingly distant worlds of history or policy making were not so distant—that these things directly impacted their lives and the lives of others in their families and communities.

My identity changed in my final years as a classroom teacher. I became a motivator, facilitator, and philosopher. I thought deeply about the aims of a social studies education and crafted lessons to transform students into citizens skilled in deliberation and decision making. My classes became microcosms of democracy. Ultimately, my new identity as a teacher affected my professional trajectory; I wanted to inspire and prepare others to become thriving professionals. Today I tell my preservice teachers, "Great teachers are not born that way; they make themselves great through study, practice, and reflection."

As a pinnacle of his conversion to a democratic teacher, Eric lobbied his administration to create a controversial issues elective course. The course sought to replicate democratic life through student-led deliberations of controversial policy issues. The course had no predetermined content, texts, or grading system. These aspects were decided through deliberation and voting by the students.

Eric set forth only three expectations in the course syllabus: (1) participation through respectful dialogue; (2) reading and annotating texts before discussions; and (3) writing reflections. Students researched, selected, and discussed a variety of issues, including the legalization of marijuana, lowering the drinking age, the right to protest at funerals, and the criminalization of abortion. Students from across the political and socioeconomic spectrum engaged one another in discussion that often continued into hallways, buses, and homes. See Moffa (2018) for a detailed account of the course.

A MODEL FOR PROFESSIONAL GROWTH

While the ill effects of NCLB have been moderated through revamped federal legislation, the standards-based and high-stakes testing era remains the dominant paradigm of public education in the United States. The Every Student Succeeds Act (2015), the federal law that replaced NCLB, still exemplifies top-down policy mandates that retain annual standardized testing requirements.

Concurrently, teachers in states like West Virginia continue to work under a political environment of statewide debates over educational reforms. One controversial legislative act, passed during a special summer session when teachers' strike power was diminished, enabled the first charter schools in the state. These political contexts stimulate the need for conscientious teachers who build the capacity to retain and grow their professional autonomy, voice, and purposes.

In spite of external political pressures from both federal and state legislatures, our early career experiences produced pathways for professional growth that enabled us to thrive. Reflecting on our professional experiences and relationship led us to create a model for growth that could be adapted by other educators looking to thrive while facing similar threats to their autonomy and voice. The following list highlights six specific areas that stimulated growth for us, each rooted in our own professional experiences:

Be selectively subversive. Teachers are professionals. Professionals abide by a code of ethics and a standard of high achievement. Yet when faced with political control external to their professional expertise of teaching and learning, it is the duty of the teacher to be consciously subversive—or, in other words, to be autonomously professional. This does not mean to enact a flagrant disregard of laws, but it means putting students' needs first despite the standards and testing regimen that might be externally imposed.

Network. Teachers' work is often done away from the eyes of other professionals. Great teachers know the benefits of collaboration and the mutual exchange of ideas. While some schools and districts will have formal mentoring structures, teachers should seek networks of like-minded educators. Attending institutes, workshops, and conferences can help a teacher envision a professional life that might otherwise never arise if they remain in a solitary state.

Take initiative. If limited access to professional development and networks exist, teachers should become the stimulus for professional development with their colleagues, perhaps through either formal or informal PLCs. Eric fostered the understanding of new tools and ideas among his social studies colleagues as a result of attending AP training sessions.

Every teacher is a teacher leader. Teachers might be ignoring or avoiding it, but every teacher is a teacher-leader. Every teacher contributes to the culture of a school and the profession. One's willingness to engage, inspire, and lead is the linchpin for driving a school, and the profession at large, forward against animosity it encounters. Owning one's role as a teacher leader should lead to gravitating toward influential opportunities across different levels of control of schooling.

Study your trade. Effective teaching is not a purely natural act. A teacher should continuously reflect on their skills, disposition, curriculum, and instructional strategies. Teachers should consider the benefits of further academic or autodidactic efforts regarding curriculum and instruction, and put this learning into practice in their classroom.

Be a public messenger. Schools are often under attack by politicians who fail to understand the purpose or passion of great teachers. While humility is a virtue, teachers should recognize the power in seeking and receiving accolades, publicity, and prestige, which enables them to put on public display their inspiring and difficult work. This type of public messaging may begin to change the sometimes negative narrative around teaching.

In an era of extreme challenges, we were able to garner support from one another to make informed professional choices for our students and ourselves, moving from surviving to thriving in our classrooms. We both learned that what we included in our curricula showed our students what we valued. Successful educators value their own learning as much as their students' and when educators engage in quality professional development, and invest in themselves, they can become the teacher that both educates and advocates for their students and their profession in the complex landscape of education.

REFERENCES

Associated Press. (2009, November 9). State takes over Grant County schools. *The Register-Herald.* Retrieved from https://www.register-herald.com/news/state_and__region/state-takes-over-grant-county-schools/article_5f551b77-7d0f-53b8-82d0-887d87b0b2dd.html

Au, W. (2007). High-stakes testing and curricular control: A qualitative metasynthesis. *Educational Researcher, 36*(5), 258–267.

Beers, K., & Probst, R. E. (2017). *Disrupting thinking: Why how we read matters.* New York, NY: Scholastic Inc.

Beijaard, D., Meijer, P. C., & Verloop, N. (2004). Reconsidering research on teachers' professional identity. *Teaching and Teacher Education, 20*(2), 107–128.

Berryhill, J., Linney, J. A., & Fromewick, J. (2009). The effects of education accountability on teachers: Are policies too stress-provoking for their own good? *International Journal of Education Policy and Leadership, 4*(5), 1–14.

Cavanagh, S. (2012, March 8). Survey: N.C. teachers say high-stakes tests dominate classes. *Education Week.* Retrieved from http://blogs.edweek.org/edweek/state_edwatch/2012/03/survey_nc_teachers_dissatisfied_with_high-stakes_tests.html?cmp=ENL-EU-NEWS2

CIRCLE. (2014). A national survey of civics and U.S. government teachers. Retrieved from https://civicyouth.org/how-civics-is-taught-in-america-a-national-survey-of-civics-and-u-s-government-teachers/

Common Core State Standards Initiative (2019). English Language Arts Standards, History/Social Studies, Grades 11–12. Retrieved from http://www.corestandards.org/ELA-Literacy/RH/11-12/

Evans, R. W. (2001). Thoughts on redirecting a runaway train: A critique of the standards movement. *Theory & Research in Social Education, 29*(2), 330–339.

Evans, R. W. (2004). *The social studies wars: What should we teach the children?* New York, NY: Teachers College Press.

Every Student Succeeds Act of 2015, Pub. L. No. 114–95 § 114 Stat. 1177 (2015-2016).

Gallagher, K. (2015). *In the best interest of students: Staying true to what works in the ELA classroom.* Portland, ME: Stenhouse Publishers.

Grissom, J. A., Nicholson-Crotty, S., & Harrington, J. R. (2014). Estimating the effects of No Child Left Behind on teachers' work environments and job attitudes. *Educational Evaluation and Policy Analysis, 36*(4), 417–436.

Gruenewald, D. A. (2003). The best of both worlds: A critical pedagogy of place. *Educational Researcher, 32*(4), 3–12.

Hess, D. E. (2009). *Controversy in the classroom: The democratic power of discussion.* New York, NY: Routledge.

Kardos, S. M., & Johnson, S. M. (2007). On their own and presumed expert: New teachers' experience with their colleagues. *Teachers College Record, 109*(9), 2083–2106.

Lesh, B. (2011). *Why don't you just tell us the answer? Teaching historical thinking in grades 7–12.* Portland, ME: Stenhouse Publishers.

Moe, T. M. (2003). Politics, control, and the future of school accountability. In P. E. Peterson & M. R. West (Eds.), *No child left behind? The politics and practice of school accountability* (pp. 80–106). Washington, DC: Brookings Institution Press.

Moffa, E. D. (2018). Build your own course: Creating a controversial issues class at one Appalachian high school. In L. Wilcox & C. Brant (Eds.), *It's being done in social studies: Race, class, gender and sexuality in the pre/K–12 curriculum* (pp. 157–168). Charlotte, NC: Information Age Publishing.

National Council of Teachers of English, & International Reading Association (Eds). (1996). *Standards for the English language arts.* Newark, DE/Urbana, IL: International Reading Association/National Council of Teachers of English.

No Child Left Behind Act of 2002, P.L. 107–110, 20 U.S.C. § 6319 (2002).

Poling, T. M. (2018, April 2). Why one West Virginia teacher of the year stood on the picket lines. *Education Week.* Retrieved from https://blogs.edweek.org/teachers/teacher_leader_voices/2018/04/this_is_why_i_walked_why_one_w.html

Torney-Purta, J. (2002). The school's role in developing civic engagement: A study of adolescents in twenty-eight countries. *Applied Developmental Science, 6*(4), 203–212.

Valentine, J. (2007). The instructional practices inventory: Using a student learning assessment to foster organizational learning. *Middle Level Leadership Center.* Retrieved from https://mospace.umsystem.edu/xmlui/handle/10355/3565

Vinson, K. D. (1999). National curriculum standards and social studies education: Dewey, Freire, Foucault, and the construction of a radical critique. *Theory & Research in Social Education, 27*(3), 296–328.

Westheimer, J., & Kahne, J. (2004). What kind of citizen? The politics of educating for democracy. *American Educational Research Journal, 41*(2), 237–269.

Chapter Eight

Sustaining Our Voices

Critical Collaboration through English Teacher Communities of Practice

Kristen Pastore-Capuana and Deborah Bertlesman

> "Don't tell me I can't rise and crash. We're breaking the shore you've shaped us into."—excerpt from "Untamable Force"

The stanza above comes from a poem performed by three first-year participants at the Youth Voices Conference, an event that showcases student work from many grade 7–12 English language arts classrooms within one local community. The three ninth grade students and Deborah (Deb) Bertlesman, their English teacher, stood at the front of a packed room of parents, fellow classmates, teacher candidates, local English language arts teachers, and friends on a May afternoon in 2018. Since 2015, this co-developed event by the Western New York Network of English Teachers (WNYNET) and the SUNY Buffalo State English education program seeks to reclaim space for the voices of youth in their schools and communities while repositioning English language arts classrooms as places of meaning, purpose, and power.

The three youth poets, Leslie, Aliyah, and Fatimah, performed a spoken word piece that they had been writing, editing, and rehearsing for a month. Their voices echoed in unison, "Women are like oceans. Look into her eyes and you'll see the empowering waves crash against the limits that have been set." The roots of this poem grew from the students each investigating and writing a research paper that addressed gender inequality. Leslie examined women in athletics, Aliyah researched women in the workforce, and Fatimah studied women in education.

The three decided to present their work at Youth Voices. Their individual research projects evolved into a collaborative spoken word poem using the conceit of women as oceans. As their Youth Voices session concluded, Deb heard an English education teacher candidate remark, "So this is what this is all really about. I want to be a part of that." The audience's response and the teacher candidate's comment encapsulate our beliefs about the power of English education.

The moment described above was the culmination of rich classroom critical literacy experiences, students' lived experiences as curriculum, and compositional opportunities focused on revision and publication with an authentic audience. All of this occurred within a teaching context that did not overtly privilege teacher curricular autonomy. Teachers, including Deb, were instructed to use the EngageNY scripted modules for the year's units. This was a policy all English teachers had to face in Deb's large urban school district.

Deb argues that her ability to sustain her work over the last eight years was her immersion in a local English teacher network and the relationships she had fostered with colleagues outside of her district and at SUNY Buffalo State. One of these colleagues is coauthor Kristen Pastore-Capuana, an assistant professor of English Education at SUNY Buffalo State, colleague in WNYNET, and former mentor teacher.

Being a part of this community supported Deb as she sometimes has to teach "with the door closed" in order to advocate for curricula that authentically address the needs and interests of her students. Similarly, Kristen's relationship with Deb informed Kristen's work with teacher candidates as they collaborate on many professional development events, including the evolution of the Youth Voices Conference.

This chapter will explore how our participation in an English teacher, teacher educator, and English language arts student community of practice (Lave and Wenger, 1991) cultivated opportunities for both professional growth and innovative curricular change in the face of national and local pressures for standardization.

KRISTEN'S TEACHING STORY

Growing up, Kristen resisted the idea of becoming a teacher even though her family and friends frequently voiced that it would be the perfect professional fit for her. Although she was an English major in college and not involved in any education programs, she did participate in Boston College's 4Boston program. During this time she tutored at an after-school program in a Boston housing community and spent two years working with elementary and middle school youth. Reflecting on her collegiate experience, she realized that participating in 4Boston was a transformative experience and decided to pursue a teaching certification.

Her English language arts 7–12 teaching certification and master's degree at the University at Buffalo connected her with Dr. James Cercone (Jim). While a new teacher, Kristen student taught and became a colleague with Jim at Cheektowaga Central High School, a first-ring suburban high school in western New York. As a new teacher, she was able to see firsthand what a critical inquiry stance (Freire, 1972; Haddix, 2009; Kinloch, 2010) looked like in practice.

Jim and Kristen collaborated to develop curriculum and partnered with the University at Buffalo for initiatives around digital video, an introduction to education course for high school students, elective programming, and inquiry-based teaching presentations for National Council of Teachers of English (NCTE) conferences. This partnership continued over the next sixteen years and Kristen and Jim are now English education colleagues at SUNY Buffalo State.

While teaching high school, Kristen experienced the impact of both NCLB and Race to the Top educational policies on teachers and students. In 2012, changes in measuring teacher efficacy were rolled out and many schools, including the one where Kristen taught, were shifting to the new Common Core Learning Standards (CCLS). Although Kristen and her colleagues faced pressure to enact scripted curriculum, they argued against the modules and created curriculum that aligned with CCLS and met the needs of their students.

At that time, Kristen also was working with Deb Bertlesman for her field observations and student teaching. From the start, Deb was a collaborator in the classroom with a commitment to critical inquiry–based teaching practices. Deb met Jim when he was her methods professor at the University at Buffalo. She cites his influence as grounding her in social justice pedagogy.

Although the mentor teacher–student teacher power dynamic is often characterized as top-down, Kristen saw Deb as a colleague who not only was able to discuss progressive approaches to English teaching at a time when modules were being introduced but also was connected to a teacher education program that valued similar instructional approaches.

These conversations continued as we worked together through WNYNET to create professional development events, youth conferences, and innovative English education coursework.

KRISTEN'S NARRATIVE

Leaving the high school classroom was one of the most difficult decisions of my life. Although it was challenging at times, teaching English language arts for fourteen years altered me as a human being in ways that I never imagined. I am not the same person I was before I became a teacher. Who could be? It was an honor to bear witness to the stories of my students and see how their lived experiences, the texts we read, and the words we authored took new shapes that we created across a school year.

Tears streamed down my face as I carried my boxes, plants, classroom library, lights, and archived student work into my car on my final day. As I walked out of the door, one of my colleagues said, "Don't forget about us." The college where I was going to teach was only twelve miles away, but it felt like I was traveling to another planet.

As I transitioned to teacher education, I was able to participate more in WNYNET meetings and work with in-service teacher leaders to create new visions for professional development and plan events like Youth Voices. I attended monthly meetings where I was able to be with Deb Bertlesman often. Deb is a force of nature, and I loved hearing her stories about her students and their critical work. As a student teacher in my classroom, Deb demonstrated a keen eye for connecting with students and engaging them in critical conversations. Years later, Deb became a frequent speaker in my methods courses and constantly challenged me to think about the ways in which I was engaging my teacher candidates in inquiry teaching.

My relationship with Deb and WNYNET remind me of Lilla Watson's quote: "If you have come here to help me you are wasting your time, but if you have come because your liberation is bound up with mine, then let us work together." Teacher education should not be another planet; we need to be shoulder to shoulder with folks in classrooms. We need to listen and learn more from teachers like Deb who are doing important work, every period of every school day. Deb has become one of my north stars in this field, and I feel comforted that our work is stronger because we are truly in this together.

DEB'S TEACHING STORY

After obtaining an English degree with a concentration in creative writing, Deb worked at Gay and Lesbian Youth Services of Western New York (GLYS), where she led spoken word writing workshops while pursuing her teaching certification. After student teaching in diverse settings, she was hired by a small private Catholic school with a predominantly middle class and white student population. Reflecting on her initial teaching experiences, Deb decided that she wanted to dedicate her career to urban education to be able to continue to work in schools where student voices rose from a variety of backgrounds. Deb was soon hired in a large urban school district in western New York.

At the beginning of her teaching career, she was immediately involved with WNYNET. Through this experience, she stayed connected to the critical literacy and inquiry frameworks first presented to her as a graduate student. After attending meetings for about a year, Deb was nominated to be president of the organization.

As a teacher in a large urban district where certain schools were labeled by the state as "failing," the district became involved in top-down reform efforts to improve student performance on state tests and other measures of accountability. One of the efforts was to make it mandatory that English teachers throughout the district abide by the New York State Modules. The modules, a scripted curriculum, provide teachers with required texts, questions, assessments, and example student responses that teachers are required to follow. This constricting curriculum creates a contradictory space for teachers who believe in the critical, inquiry-based pedagogy at the core of WNYNET.

Deb was hired not at a failing school but a school that stated it supported the creative endeavors of students as a core part of its mission. Despite this, all English teachers were still required to follow to the modules, a stipulation that is not seen at more affluent local suburban schools. Deb creates space within the New York State modules to prioritize student choice, voice, and empowerment. She allows students to take on critical, inquiry-based perspectives while thwarting the New Criticism framework presented in the curriculum (Tampio, 2018) and lack of representation in suggested text exemplars (Schieble, 2014).

DEB'S NARRATIVE

Although I am certainly not immune to the emotional and professional weights of top-down reform, I have never truly worked alone. As a graduate student, I had a professor who supported my thinking and learning continuously outside of class. As a student teacher, my cooperating teacher was truly a mentor who, in many ways, relinquished her expertly curated classroom community to a hopeful neophyte. In teaching, I have been continuously supported by a network of English teachers that I worked with my mentors to create.

The first time I met Kristen, my soon to be cooperating teacher, she was presenting at the first summer conference hosted by WNYNET. Although WNYNET was still a new organization at the time of Kristen's presentation, it has grown into something much more powerful. Kristen's talk was centered on the idea of reclaiming the English classroom. She described top-down reforms as Orwellian and called all teachers to take back their classrooms for students.

The first time I met my cooperating teacher, she was positioned as an expert in front of a room of working professionals. She was not speaking about standards or test scores. She was giving me a glimpse into the most important space I would enter. Student teaching with Kristen pushed me to continuously evaluate my goals as an educator, but there were foundational understandings that never changed. I was not in Kristen's classroom to teach to a test. I was learning how to get kids to do meaningful work, grounded in social justice and critical consciousness.

The relationship that began through student teaching would continue through the induction phase of my career. The first five years of teaching have been proven to be critical moments in developing teacher identity. Some teachers enter the field and fall to standardized, scripted curricula focused on testable skills. Others feel overwhelmed and unsupported and end up leaving the profession. In the first five years of my teaching, I was connected to my university professor, Dr. James Cercone (Jim), and my cooperating teacher, Kristen, who was working on her PhD.

Some of the conversations were expected. I emailed them for resources and asked about my lesson plans. During this time, we also worked to continue to build WNYNET. We all presented at different WNYNET conferences, supported new teachers, and developed a regional voice as experts in our field. More importantly, I called them crying. I called Jim and Kristen, both of them separately, when I received a counseling note in my file for questioning test-based assessments in a strictly scripted curriculum. I called Jim and Kristen when I made mistakes as a new teacher. Perhaps, most importantly, I spoke with Jim and Kristen when my students succeeded in ways that we deemed important, that my students felt were important.

These moments were the things I held onto amongst conversations surrounding Data Driven Instruction based on multiple choice assessments and formulaic, insincere, writing. These conversations were the only reason I survived. Through relationships established with Jim and Kristen early on in my career, I was better able to provide my students with a space to be recognized and praised for the importance of the work that they did in their English class.

RESISTING THE PRESSURES OF MANDATED CURRICULUM

Teachers like us continue to face large-scale, national reform movements, referred to as top-down reform in recent scholarship, and localized pushes for increased standardization. As a result, many teachers and students continue to face pressures to define learning through the contexts of high-stakes national assessments and narrow definitions of literacy that promote traditional teaching focused on transmission models of instruction (Applebee, 1993; Freire, 1972; Hillocks, 2002).

Limited definitions of literacy continue to drive English language arts teaching and assessment in schools, and both novice and experienced teachers face pressure to enact more traditional models of instruction dominated by canonical texts and the printed word (Kelchtermans & Ballet, 2002; Smagorinsky et al., 2013). This narrowing of curricular space through high stakes assessment and mandated curricula impacts schools already facing structural inequalities, opportunity gaps, and evaluative measures tied to school funding. Deb's district continues to face pressures to make Adequate Yearly Progress (AYP) as measured by state test scores and local ranking systems such as Business First, which perpetuate limited representations of city students, teachers, and the community at large.

Furthermore, in the first few years of teaching under these reform efforts, feelings of loneliness and failure increase (Darling-Hammond, 1999; Freedman & Appleman, 2008; Ingersoll, 2001, 2003, 2004), often causing teachers to leave the profession. WNYNET was created as a space for teachers to discuss these tensions within their teaching contexts and advocate for progressive pedagogy and teacher autonomy. Although we continued our professional relationship after Deb's student teaching placement, WNYNET became a space for professional collaboration with a reach beyond our individual classrooms.

THE POWER OF WNYNET

WNYNET began in 2012 with a group of Jim's graduate school classmates who had recently entered the field. They kept in contact with each other and Jim, and expressed concerns about their early experiences in the classroom. At that time, probationary English language arts teaching positions were scarce; new teachers missed the rich discussions around pedagogy and practice and felt isolated. Simultaneously, local teachers faced new pressures from the shift to CCLS and teacher evaluations tied to standardized testing performance.

In an effort to stay more formally connected, the students attempted to create an alumni group. When that failed to come to fruition, they began WNYNET as an independent, nonprofit organization. Deb was first introduced to the organization when a member walked into her graduate class with flyers to attend a meeting. When WNYNET planned their first summer professional development event in 2012, they invited Kristen to do a talk entitled "Reclaiming English Language Arts Teaching," which discussed teacher agency in the era of neoliberal education reform.

Over the next couple of years, WNYNET grew into a not-for-profit, teacher-driven professional organization and social network focused on encouraging and supporting meaningful teaching of English language arts in the greater Buffalo-Niagara region (Cercone, 2009, 2014). WNYNET advocates for inquiry-based (Beach & Myers, 2001; Fecho, 2004; Gustavson, 2007) models of literacy instruction that draw from work on cultural studies (Fecho & Clifton, 2016; Gaughan, 1998), critical literacy (Freire, 1972; Haddix, 2009; Kinloch, 2010), and reading and writing workshop approaches in secondary classrooms (Atwell, 2014; Hicks, 2009).

Since 2013, WNYNET has been housed in the SUNY Buffalo State English education program, where Jim and Kristen teach, and together they are conceived of as a regional hub for English teaching in western New York. These organizations seek to create powerful learning opportunities for teacher candidates through relevant coursework and clinically rich classroom experiences, while advocating and supporting in-service teachers throughout their careers. WNYNET situates itself in sociocultural perspectives on teaching and learning for a long-term, systemic approach that provides preservice and in-service teachers with meaningful learning opportunities and ongoing support throughout their careers.

Referring to initial learning within these communities as "legitimate peripheral participation," they sought to explain how new participants work on the periphery of a given practice and over time become full participants within that practice. Wenger (1998) has since explored the concept in greater detail, examining how "newcomers" learn through participation and interactions with "old-timers" of a given practice.

WNYNET conceptualizes the "newcomer" and "old-timer" relationship as reciprocal, positioning both members as valued experts and learners across participatory spaces. In our case, we have both "newcomer" and "old-timer" roles in the larger community of practice and in our own personal relationship. For example, Deb has reached out to Kristen to talk through situations at her school regarding when and how to advocate for independent reading initiatives and more authentic district-based assessments. Kristen has asked Deb to share her experiences as an English teacher facing scripted curricula pressures to better understand what her teacher candidates need as they enter local classrooms.

We collaborate through WNYNET sponsored, "classroom-up" (Cercone, 2009) professional development conferences and related activities for in-service teachers and teacher candidates. The organization developed a sense of community over several types of events that allowed members to interact in different ways.

WNYNET has grown to include a large online social network, increased professional development offerings, teacher awards, and social events; however, the organization still faces challenges as it continues to grow in the region. The organization is run by working professionals in secondary schools and teacher education programs who are not compensated for their time or efforts. Deb is currently the president of WNYNET, and Kristen is the assistant director; they work closely as colleagues at monthly meetings and on the organization's educational initiatives.

WNYNET struggled to be independent from an existing educational entity, and although SUNY Buffalo State provides space for events, the organization does not receive formal funding from the college. The organization continues to explore ways to support participation from more in-service teachers who are already faced with busy teaching schedules and professional pressures. These issues present challenges to the sustainability of an organization dependent on the investment of time from teachers and teacher educators.

YOUTH VOICES CONFERENCE

In the summer of 2014, a group of teachers, which included us, met informally through WNYNET to develop an inquiry unit exploring the teenage experience and teenage engagement in community-based civic change. Teachers brainstormed texts to read and analyze, composing experiences and potential assessments to explore these questions. During this conversation, an idea emerged about bringing the students from these different classrooms together in the spring to share the projects that came out of this shared curriculum planning.

In April of the next year, English teachers and their students participated in the first Youth Voices Speaker Series. Approximately thirty students participated and shared projects stemming from cultural identity exploration to the pressures on modern students and schools. Participants all crowded into one room at Buffalo State College to listen to students share their TED Talks, research projects, and creative poetry rooted in important social and identity issues in their communities and our world.

Conceptualized initially as a showcase of innovative student work, Youth Voices became a space for teachers and students across urban and suburban districts to meet and share their work. In a community where conversations about school districts were too often rooted in test scores performance and district rankings, Youth Voices fostered dialogue between kids sharing creative expertise rarely showcased on the news. Over the last five years, the Youth Voices Speaker Series has grown from a one-room event to the Youth Voices Conference, a four-hour conference where more than one hundred middle school and high school students from districts across rural, urban, and suburban communities in western New York, some students from the Albany area, and their English teachers share their innovative critical inquiry work.

YOUTH VOICES AND TEACHER IDENTITY DEVELOPMENT

As a high school teacher, Kristen participated in the inquiry group that planned the first Youth Voices and brought high school seniors from her Cultural Perspectives elective course to the first event. After exploring issues of the modern teenage experience and investigating social issues facing their community, Kristen's students crafted research projects that examined modern storytelling in hip-hop music, microaggressions in school, and limited standards of beauty. Students presented their work in the form of documentary films, a TED Talk that integrated QR codes for audience participation, and a research presentation with data displayed through Google Forms analytics.

For Deb, participation in Youth Voices created literacy learning opportunities for her students to grow as readers and writers while also becoming change agents in their schools. In addition to the three youth poets previously mentioned, Deb and her students were able to reimagine a unit exploring Bradbury's (1967) *Fahrenheit 451* through an inquiry into questions surrounding standing up for what we believe in, risk taking, and what it means to find our individual and collective power.

After delivering a TED Talk titled "From Influenced to Influencer: Being a Leader in the Black Community," Deb's student, Keivougn, remarked, "I know I have been an intellectual for a long time, but I was able to do something that I really cared about and have my crew with me. I did me. I was myself and I was a writer." Youth Voices became an agentive space for both Deb and her students to showcase the rich work they created in spite of standardized curricular pressures.

Over the last two years, Kristen's methods courses have increased their participation in Youth Voices and the event is an integral component of the English education program. Through the Youth Voices Mentorship Partnership in methods, teacher candidates are paired with students in Deb's high school classes as they work on their inquiry projects for the conference.

Teacher candidates introduce themselves via email and provide continuous feedback on student writing. Deb is a guest speaker in the methods course; she introduces the project and shares her instructional model to the class. We work with the teacher candidates to model how to approach writing feedback. Teacher candidates then independently work with students under our guidance.

Teacher candidates in methods visit Deb's classroom and support the presentation preparation sessions for the conference. Teacher candidates workshop documentary films with Deb's students, provide feedback on spoken word pieces, and function as potential audience members to pose potential questions to her students. On the day of the event, the teacher candidates are paired with Deb's and other local teachers' students to serve as guides for the event. The teacher candidates also help organize the specifics of the conference by running the registration table, helping set up the technology in rooms or art displays, and supporting participating teachers in any way necessary.

Following the conference, teacher candidates in the methods course reflect on their experiences in Deb's classroom and the conference through writing and discussion in class. Kristen shared videos recorded from the student work shared at the conference as a place to analyze how a critical inquiry pedagogical stance can lead to rigorous authentic assessments like the ones witnessed at Youth Voices. In a reflection assignment written after the 2019 Youth Voices Conference, Kathryn, a teacher candidate, wrote:

> The writing and presentations I saw at Youth Voices and in our time working with students this semester makes me hopeful. I am hopeful that I will be able to do this in my own classroom and knowing that it can actually be done, this isn't just something we read about in an idealistic textbook.

Transitioning to higher education was difficult to Kristen; moreover, her identity was deeply entrenched with being a high school English teacher. She moved to higher education to have the opportunity to work with teacher candidates and advocate for in-service teachers. She is, as discussed in the introduction to this book, an "invested stayer" who acknowledges that stepping out of the high school classroom was one of the most difficult decisions of her life. Through her work with Deb and other local teachers, she has been able to sustain her connection to the real lives of adolescents alongside the successes, challenges, and tensions facing in-service teachers.

THE POWER OF PROFESSIONAL RELATIONSHIPS

What began as a collaboration in a student teaching placement has evolved into a professional partnership. With the support of WNYNET and the larger community of practice, we have navigated changing landscapes and pressures in both secondary and higher education teaching contexts. While not a panacea for counteracting top-down education reform and localized pressures for standardization, professional relationships mitigate feelings of loneliness and support teachers in advocating for curriculum they feel their students deserve.

Although our relationship led to many conversations about teaching and learning, participation in WNYNET and the larger community of practice facilitated more opportunities to engage in reflection on teaching, plan professional development events, and connect with other teachers across diverse contexts to better understand the educational landscape of their community.

Participation in the initial creation and continued development of the Youth Voices Conference provided both of us a space to collaborate on curriculum and reinforce research-based practices that were not always privileged in school-district contexts. The conference itself became a new model for authentic, multimodal assessment rooted in student identities and community justice issues. English language arts curriculum that was not overtly privileged in some local classrooms was celebrated at Youth Voices. The conference is a space for both teachers and students to exercise their voices with a community ready to listen. Youth Voices represents a new model for professional development. WNYNET and the Buffalo State English Education program have developed Youth Voices into a year-long professional development experience where teachers meet throughout the fall and winter to work on inquiry-based instructional models that can lead to Youth Voices projects and presentations.

Teachers and teacher educators are more powerful together. Our professional relationship and participation in local communities of practice helped us navigate challenging moments in our careers while supporting the creation of new programming that impacted local teachers, students, and teacher candidates. Moving beyond just professional camaraderie and emotional support, relationships between teachers and teacher educators create opportunities to reclaim spaces to enact meaningful English language arts teaching that crosses boundaries to empower and redefine.

REFERENCES

Applebee, A. (1993). *Curriculum as conversation: Transforming traditions of teaching and learning.* Chicago, IL: University of Chicago Press.

Atwell, N. (2014). *In the middle: Writing, reading, and learning with adolescents.* Upper Montclair, NJ: Boynton/Cook.

Beach, R., & Myers, J. (2001). *Inquiry-based English instruction: Engaging students in life and literature.* New York: Teachers College Press.

Bradbury, R. (1967). *Fahrenheit 451.* New York, NY: Simon and Schuster.

Cercone, J. (2009). We're smarter together: Building professional social networks in English education. *English Education, 41*(3), 199–206.

Cercone, J. (2014). Communities of practice: Bridging the gap between methods courses and secondary schools. In J. Brass & A. Webb (Eds.), *Reclaiming English Language Arts Methods Courses: Critical Issues and Challenges for Teacher Educators in Top Down Times* (109–122). New York, NY: Routledge.

Darling-Hammond, L. (1999). Target time toward teachers. *Journal of Staff Development, 20*(2), 31–36.

Fecho, B., & Clifton, J. (2016). *Dialoguing across cultures, identities, and learning: Crosscurrents and complexities in literacy classrooms.* Taylor & Francis.

Freedman, S. W., & Appleman, D. (2008). "What else would I be doing?": Teacher identity and teacher retention in urban schools. *Teacher Education Quarterly, 35*(3), 109–126.

Freire, P. (1972). *Pedagogy of the oppressed.* New York, NY: Herder and Herder.

Gaughan, J. (1998). *Cultural reflections: Critical teaching and learning in the English classroom.* Portsmouth, NH: Boynton/Cook Publishers.

Gustavson, L. (2007). *Youth learning on their own terms: Creative practices and classroom teaching* (Critical youth studies). New York, NY: Routledge.

Haddix, M. (2009). Black boys can write: Challenging dominant framings of African American adolescent males in literacy research. *Journal of Adolescent & Adult Literacy, 53*(4), 341–343.

Hicks, T. (2009). *The digital writing workshop.* Portsmouth, NH: Heinemann.

Hillocks, G., Jr. (2002). *The testing trap: How state writing assessments control learning* (Language and literacy series). New York, NY: Teachers College Press.

Ingersoll, R. (2001). Teacher turnover and teacher shortages: An organizational analysis. *American Educational Research Journal, 38*(3), 499–534.

Ingersoll, R. (2003). *Is there really a teacher shortage?* (a research report co-sponsored by the Center for the Study of Teaching and Policy and the Consortium for Policy Work in education; Document R-03-04). Seattle, WA: Center for the Study of Teaching and Policy at the University of Washington.

Ingersoll, R. (2004). "Why do high-poverty schools have difficulty staffing their classrooms with qualified teachers?" Report prepared for Renewing Our Schools, Securing Our Future, a National Task Force on Public Education, Center for American Progress, Institute for America's Future.

Kelchtermans, G., & Ballet, K. (2002). The micropolitics of teacher induction: A narrative-biographical study on teacher socialization. *Teaching and Teacher Education, 18*(1), 105–120.

Kinloch, V. (2010). *Harlem on our minds.* New York, NY: Teachers College Press.

Lave, J., & Wenger, E. (1991). *Situated learning: Legitimate peripheral participation.* Cambridge, UK: Cambridge University Press.

Schieble, M. (2014). Reframing equity under Common Core: A commentary on the text exemplar list for grades 9-12. *English Teaching: Practice & Critique (University of Waikato), 13*(1), 155–168. Retrieved from http://search.ebscohost.com/login.aspx?direct=true&db=eue&AN=108365439&site=ehost-live&scope=site

Smagorinsky, P., Rhym, D., & Moore, C. P. (2013). Competing centers of gravity: A beginning English teacher's socialization process within conflictual settings. *English Education, 45*(2), 147–182.

Tampio, N. (2018). A Democratic Critique of the Common Core English Language Arts (ELA) Standards. *Democracy & Education, 26*(1), 1–7. Retrieved from http://search.ebscohost.com/login.aspx?direct=true&db=eue&AN=129378759&site=ehost-live&scope=site

Wenger, E. (1998). Communities of practice: Learning as a social system. *Systems Thinker, 9*(5), 2–3.

III

Disciplinary Landscapes

Chapter Nine

Persisting in Teaching with a New Vision of Science Education

Elizabeth Xeng de los Santos, Candice Guy-Gaytán, and Sylvia Scoggin

Imagine the following scenario: You have been teaching high school science for the past twenty years. You thought you were doing a good job. You design hands-on and inquiry-based lessons, your students are mostly engaged and well-behaved, and you receive excellent or satisfactory ratings on your teaching evaluations every year. You have developed rules and routines that work for your classroom and have file cabinets full of your favorite activities and labs. Your students know what to expect in your science class.

Then your state adopts the Next Generation Science Standards (NGSS) and you feel as if almost everything you know about science teaching has figuratively gone out the window. Now there are three dimensions—disciplinary core ideas, scientific and engineering practices, and crosscutting concepts—that should be integrated in your instruction. You may recognize the core ideas and practices but are unsure about what the crosscutting concepts are and how they fit with the other two dimensions.

The new standards are written in the form of three-dimensional performance expectations that are grouped into familiar-looking topic arrangements such as weather and climate, chemical reactions, or natural selection and evolution; however, you struggle to understand how the performance expectations translate into everyday lessons and activities. You also learn that lessons should be phenomenon based, but you are confused about what counts as a phenomenon. You attend professional development to learn more about NGSS but, at the end of the day, you wonder how you will enact this new vision of science education with the limited time and resources available to you. Although the three dimensions of NGSS are displayed on posters in your classroom, you return often to the trusted materials in your file cabinet.

FACING THE CHALLENGING INSTRUCTIONAL SHIFTS CALLED FOR IN NGSS

This scenario may sound familiar to veteran and early-career teachers alike. Veteran teachers may have spent the entirety of their careers using the *National Science Education Standards* (National Research Council, 1996), but the *Framework for K–12 Science Education* (National Research Council, 2012) and *Next Generation Science Standards* (Next Generation Science Standards Lead States, 2013) have presented a call for a radical shift in teaching practices from what has been termed "traditional science teaching." New teachers most likely experienced traditional modes of instruction as K–12 students and may feel that their preservice education did not adequately prepare them for NGSS.

Science teachers currently face the challenge of learning new instructional practices, in part because they have not experienced an NGSS classroom as students or teachers. Furthermore, the current lack of quality NGSS curricular resources across K–12 makes implementation even more daunting. Reform documents call for a reconceptualization of teaching and learning from (1) *learning about* science topics to *figuring out* phenomena (Schwarz et al., 2017); (2) teachers holding disciplinary authority to students developing epistemic authority and agency; and (3) teachers relying primarily on summative assessments to integrating assessment and instruction (National Academies of Sciences, Engineering, and Medicine, 2017).

Ultimately, these shifts challenge teachers to reenvision their roles in the classroom as designers of learning experiences that engage all students equitably in three-dimensional science learning, defined as the integration of scientific and engineering practices, disciplinary core ideas, and crosscutting concepts. Reimagining roles for three-dimensional science learning requires consideration of students' epistemic agency, or their authority to shape the practice and knowledge as a community of learners (Miller et al., 2018; Roehl, 2012; Stroupe, 2014), which is a vastly different view of students' roles from the traditional positioning of students as passive receivers of knowledge through lecture, notetaking, and "cookbook" laboratory activities.

The integration of assessment and instruction means making students' thinking visible so that instruction builds on the resources that students bring with them to the classroom, expanding on their prior knowledge and experiences. Consequently, NGSS articulates a new vision of science education that is challenging for many teachers to understand and enact. For experienced teachers, NGSS truly represents a paradigm shift considering that it has been twenty years since the publication of the last standards, the *National Science Education Standards* (National Research Council, 1996).

In this chapter, we share our experiences collaborating on a district-wide initiative to support teachers' implementation of NGSS in northern Nevada. We discuss how our continually evolving collaboration has helped us recognize the unique contributions we have made in supporting one another to persevere in this changing educational landscape and hope that our approach to supporting NGSS implementation may help others consider the valuable roles they can play in supporting their teaching communities to continue the important work of providing equitable science learning opportunities for all students.

DEVELOPING A RESEARCH-PRACTICE-PARTNERSHIP TO SUPPORT SCIENCE EDUCATION IN NORTHERN NEVADA

Although the Nevada State Department of Education adopted NGSS in 2013, funding for professional development was limited. When NGSS was introduced to teachers in our school district during the 2013–2014 school year, both new and veteran teachers were skeptical. A majority adopted the attitude of "this too shall pass" and continued teaching using the lesson plans they knew to be successful with their students. A few accepted the philosophical basis of the new standards, but even they felt the standards were impossible to implement—that they represented a "pie in the sky" dream.

Still others were vehemently opposed to the standards because they felt they would not prepare students for "the real world" of college and post–high school work. With no NGSS-aligned curricular resources or trainers with expertise in the standards, the job of rolling out NGSS fell to a limited number of science coordinators in districts throughout the state. The job was overwhelming, and even teachers who saw the value in shifting toward a classroom where students are sense-makers rather than memorizers were feeling defeated. It was then that Elizabeth and Candice came to work at the local university in 2017 as tenure-track faculty members.

In their roles as assistant professors of science education, Elizabeth and Candice aimed to provide hope for local teachers who wanted to learn how to transform their classrooms and lent credibility to some of the work that Sylvia, the district's secondary science program facilitator, had been doing to support science teachers in implementing NGSS. Both Elizabeth and Candice had experience working on NGSS-aligned curriculum development and implementation projects funded by the National Science Foundation and brought concrete examples, co-created with teachers, of what NGSS could look like in the classroom (https://carbontime.bscs.org and https://www.modelbasedbiology.com, respectively).

As former science teachers themselves, Elizabeth and Candice had a commitment to working *with* practitioners on problems of practice and wanted to first build trust and relationships with local district personnel in order to effect change in their new community. They were grateful that Sylvia was open to sharing her expertise as a district science coordinator and former classroom teacher, insights and historical knowledge of local and state policies and procedures, and extensive network of science educators.

SYLVIA'S PERSPECTIVE

How do teachers persist in teaching when we feel overwhelmed? We seek out collaborative opportunities; these could be professional learning opportunities or conversations with colleagues. When the NGSS standards were first introduced to us, I felt my world was turned upside down. It took multiple conversations with like-minded teachers to even superficially understand the shifts described in the literature we read together. I worked for hours with a colleague to plan out one unit we felt met the NGSS requirements. It was exhausting and frankly, terrifying, to change our teaching structure so drastically. That year we taught only one unit built specifically with NGSS in mind. This was when we met Elizabeth and Candice from the university; they represented a greater fount of knowledge from which we could learn. They were the missing pieces in our puzzle, the new members of our collaborative team so we could persist in our journey toward shifting our instruction to meet the needs of today's students.

It quickly became clear that the work of improving science instruction required a different way of thinking about research and practice. The concept of collaboration underlying research-practice partnerships (RPPs) provided a model for how we could work together to promote large-scale change across the district. RPPs differ from conventional ways researchers, district leaders, and teachers have previously worked together and are defined as long-term, mutualistic collaborations that use intentional strategies to foster partnership and focus on problems of practice with the goal of producing original research analyses (Coburn et al., 2013).

For example, in a traditional university-school partnership, one group may hold the authority for setting the agenda; however, a commitment to mutualism within RPPs means that priorities for partnership activities are *jointly negotiated* to help ensure that different perspectives contribute to the focus of the work:

> By working closely with researchers, district leaders can clarify their goals and gain insights into the implementation of district policies and programs. By working closely with practitioners, researchers can gain a deeper understand-

ing of classrooms, schools, and districts and just what it might take to make change. (Coburn et al., 2013, p. 3)

Thus, we set out to intentionally foster partnership activities in ways that would utilize the expertise of researchers (Elizabeth and Candice) and practitioners (Sylvia) to address important problems of practice in local settings.

Setting priorities for the partnership that benefits the work of both partners is not easy. From the practice perspective, a successful partnership requires that researchers accomplish many goals, including the following:

- provide a clear benefit to the district leader's work;
- understand the district context;
- build trust and relationships;
- be transparent about the work;
- plan for ongoing engagement; and
- be flexible and responsive (Harrison et al., 2017).

Therefore, RPPs offer a model in which researchers are committed to working *with* practitioners on mutually identified problems of practice in mutually beneficial ways.

The first step in developing an RPP is to understand the district context and build trust and relationships with district personnel, something that we had already begun. Ultimately, our collaborative construction of knowledge and development of the RPP required dialogue, trust, and intuition. These arose organically and informally from the sharing of experiences informally over drinks and breakfast meetings with plenty of coffee and sunshine. Using *Women's Ways of Knowing* (Belenky et al., 1997) as a lens to view the collaborative work they had undertaken since first meeting, we recognize that our approach to creating, nurturing, and caring for partner relationships created space for constructing knowledge, or finding "a place for reason *and* intuition *and* the expertise of others" (p. 133).

In other words, the collaborative construction of knowledge about how to improve science instruction in the district resulted from conversations among us that integrated our expertise in research and practice, intuition about what to say and when to say it, and reasoning about how to move forward with ideas and projects. Looking back over the past two years, we recognize that the partnership we have built has helped us persist in teaching and in supporting teachers to teach with a new and challenging vision of science education by showing them how they could leverage each other's expertise in mutually beneficial ways. The partnership has led to meaningful projects and presentations that have had a direct impact on science education in the district.

CANDICE'S PERSPECTIVE

As a former science teacher and current science education researcher, I have witnessed and experienced firsthand the positive influence strong relationships can have on student learning experiences: relationships between educators and their students, between educators and their curricular materials, between teachers and their colleagues and mentors, and between teachers and their administrators. I have also witnessed and experienced the exhaustion and isolation that can occur when such relationships falter or never form. This understanding has guided my continued work in education: I want to support districts, schools, and teachers in nurturing and guiding the development of relationships for equitably providing students with science learning opportunities.

However, it was in working with Elizabeth and Sylvia to jointly negotiate the priorities of our collaboration that I became aware of the relationships that I need to persist in this field. While my own work has centered on fostering relationships between others and the resources they need, I had neglected to consider the relationships that I need for my own well-being and success as a tenure-track faculty member. Not only am I dependent on my interactions and relationships with teachers and with students for my research, but I am a better researcher when I am surrounded by colleagues who genuinely care about my work and I theirs.

My interactions with Sylvia and Elizabeth have not only helped me better understand the cultural and contextual practices of educational systems and the decision-making processes for enacting policy changes in northern Nevada, but they have also helped me see how my particular expertise can play a role in influencing the widespread uptake of reform-oriented teaching practices that equitably support all learners. I look forward to seeing what our team is able to accomplish.

JOINTLY NEGOTIATING AND IDENTIFYING PROBLEMS OF PRACTICE

Next, we provide an example of how our differing expertise, roles, and responsibilities contributed to the development and implementation of a district-wide biology assessment. In 2017, after three years of working toward NGSS implementation, teachers were still unclear as to what an NGSS lesson could look like in the classroom. Knowing that Elizabeth and Candice had recently joined the faculty at the local university, Sylvia invited them each to attend one of the monthly meetings held for middle school instructional leaders and high school department leaders.

Candice presented lessons focused on the practice of modeling, a concept radically different in NGSS compared to what teachers had previously experienced. Using ideas from *Model-Based Biology: Students Making Sense of Biological Phenomena*, a yearlong suite of model-based high school biology resources, she led teachers through a sample lesson. Elizabeth led teachers through analysis of student responses to an assessment task from *Carbon TIME*, a learning-progression-based curriculum that focuses on constructing explanations of processes that transform matter and energy. Responses from teachers were overwhelmingly positive.

Building on the positive feedback from the teachers, we continued to discuss how to proceed in working with one another, holding weekly formal meetings in conference rooms on campus. Ideas were recorded and surveys were sent to all district teachers to solicit their ideas about pressing problems of practice, but nothing concrete was coming to fruition in terms of a clear path forward—that is, until Elizabeth and Sylvia began to discuss their experiences working on state-level science assessments.

Elizabeth had experience writing three-dimensional science assessment items for a large state department of education; she was also creating a short course on three-dimensional science assessment development for a regional meeting of the National Science Teaching Association (NSTA). Sylvia shared her policy insights and historical knowledge of science assessments in the state and the district.

For example, students in ninth or tenth grade (depending on the school district) must take the Nevada State High School Science Assessment for graduation. The assessment was developed after state-level adoption of NGSS. Test content is limited to life science disciplinary core ideas, associated scientific and engineering practices, and crosscutting concepts that, in theory, should be covered in all high school biology courses. However, test scores from the previous three years revealed to district teachers that their students were not as proficient in science as they would have expected.

Additionally, district administrators were becoming increasingly concerned about consistently low scores on the ACT test, which all students in Nevada must take to graduate. Although the ACT is not based on NGSS standards, the items require reasoning skills similar to what students are expected to demonstrate on the Nevada State High School Science Assessment. Thus, district administrators and teachers were invested heavily in improving students' learning experiences and, hopefully, their test scores.

Prior to NGSS, schools held testing "boot camps" where students were drilled on science content. However, teachers and administrators soon realized that this format would not be effective for assessing a student's ability to reason and apply science knowledge. According to Sylvia, teachers in the district with whom she worked closely recognized that, for students' scores to improve, students needed to experience similar items throughout the year in their classrooms.

Out of these concerns, Sylvia approached the district's director of assessment for support in developing a final semester exam aligned with NGSS that would be used district-wide to assess all students in high school biology. In subsequent conversations, it became apparent that there were extreme inequities in instruction and assessment throughout schools in the district. Termed "academic inequity" by the director, it provided the final impetus needed to gain the funds and resources necessary to begin the work of creating a common assessment for district biology classes.

Although the district assessment department had extensive knowledge in the area of assessment literacy and in developing district-wide math assessments, they lacked expertise in science content knowledge and understanding of NGSS, particularly the three-dimensional integration of disciplinary core ideas, scientific and engineering practices, and crosscutting concepts. Having spent time exploring and listening to local educators about classroom issues in the district and having experienced the NGSS assessment development process, we were well positioned to take on the task of developing the biology assessment.

Keeping to our commitment of working with teachers, we invited one biology teacher from each of the eleven comprehensive high schools in the district, the director of assessment, and an assessment consultant to participate in item writing. Candice and Elizabeth advised the development of a common final exam within the district's existing assessment system. Together, we and assessment specialists provided training in three-dimensional science assessment development for the biology teachers.

Throughout the development of the common final exam, Candice and Elizabeth observed the process, paying particular attention to the rich discussions held by the biology teachers as they wrote, reviewed, and edited assessment items. Candice and Elizabeth shared these observations with Sylvia and the assessment consultant to assist in their decision making. As of this writing, the first semester exam is complete and ready for district-wide implementation beginning in fall 2019.

In this example, the work of completing the assessment would not have been possible without our differing expertise, roles, and responsibilities. The identified problem of practice—how to support instructional shifts in teachers' practices to align with NGSS—was important for both practice and research. In Sylvia's role as secondary science program facilitator, she was responsible for supporting teachers in the district with NGSS implementation through facilitating workshops and courses and securing and distributing resources.

In Elizabeth's and Candice's roles as tenure-track faculty members with NGSS assessment expertise, we were responsible for developing and maintaining programs of research that would lead to publications and grants, products that are critical for advancing in academia. As university faculty members, we did not have the authority to determine the work of the district. However, through our partnership, we were able to jointly negotiate the development of the biology assessment.

Sylvia had the authority to take her idea to the district's director of assessment, who could then approve the project and provide needed resources, such as substitute pay for teachers to have time to write the items. Elizabeth and Candice were then afforded the opportunity to conduct a research study investigating whether and how the development and implementation of the district biology assessment influenced teachers' learning of NGSS, including potential shifts in their instruction in order to prepare their students for the exam. Research results could then contribute to the knowledge base of how to support NGSS implementation through a focus on developing teachers' three-dimensional science assessment literacy.

Engaging in this work is beneficial not only to us but also to district-level assessment personnel and the teachers involved in the assessment development process. The research study results provide empirical evidence of teacher learning that Sylvia and the director of assessment can use to justify their work and that Elizabeth and Candice can use to progress in their academic careers. The teachers benefit through having time and space to work on their understanding of NGSS in a community of learners. Throughout this work, various aspects of the assessment development process were negotiated jointly to ensure mutual benefit.

ELIZABETH'S PERSPECTIVE

Being a teacher is a core part of my professional identity. Before I pursued doctoral studies, I was a middle and high school science teacher for eleven years, and I will always identify with classroom teachers and advocate for better working conditions and learning opportunities for them. Teachers are my people! As a university professor now, I miss being in the K–12 classroom, and working with Sylvia and Candice on problems of practice that are relevant to teachers in my community has helped me persist in teaching. I believe that the vision of science education articulated in NGSS is the right path forward, and I do not think that I could persist in teaching without the companionship of like-minded science educators. I always look forward to our breakfast meetings or conversations over beer and wine; building relationships takes time and trust and is an immensely satisfying part of the work that I get to do every day. Because of the strength of the partnership that we have developed, I feel confident that we will be able to take on any challenges or opportunities that come our way.

LOOKING TOWARD THE FUTURE

> If we teach today's students as we taught yesterday's, we rob them of tomorrow.—John Dewey

Currently, teachers who are open to changes in their science instruction are driven by the idea that our world is constantly changing and, to keep up with those changes, instruction must change as well. In the past few years, the influx of technology-focused companies in northern Nevada has brought an increased focus on career readiness. Tesla's Gigafactory, which produces the battery packs for their electric vehicles, hosts a tour weekly for local middle school students. The tour guides emphasize the need for workers who are critical thinkers, which does not necessarily imply that they are college graduates.

While students dream of high-paying jobs with Tesla, their teachers hear the message that critical thinking is more important than memorizing facts in order to prepare for a future in higher education or the workplace. At the nearby Google Data Center, teachers and students on a tour hear a similar message—the company is looking for workers who can think through complex problems rather than those who need solutions presented to them.

Together, the messages from both companies highlight the importance of creating a classroom culture where students are engaged in sensemaking with the guidance of a teacher. Looking toward the future, we believe that NGSS offers a vision of science education that is challenging yet powerful and attainable for teachers and students. We plan to continue our assessment work as we support teachers in developing items for the second-semester biology final exam and potentially follow individual teachers as they navigate how to prepare their students for the new assessment. We are grateful for each other and hopeful for the future of K–12 science education in northern Nevada.

REFERENCES

Belenky, M. F., Clinchy, B. M., Goldberger, N. R., & Tarule, J. M. (1997). *Women's ways of knowing: The development of self, voice, and mind* (2nd ed.). New York, NY: Basic Books.

Coburn, C. E., Penuel, W. R., & Geil, K. E. (2013). *Research-practice partnerships: A strategy for leveraging research for educational improvement in school districts.* New York, NY: William T. Grant Foundation.

Harrison, C., Davidson, K., & Ferrell, C. (2017). Building productive relationships: District leaders' advice to researchers. *International Journal of Education Policy & Leadership, 12*(4), 1–16.

Miller, E., Manz, E., Russ, R., Stroupe, D., & Berland, L. (2018). Addressing the epistemic elephant in the room: Epistemic agency and the next generation science standards. *Journal of Research in Science Teaching, 55*(7), 1053–1075.

National Academies of Sciences, Engineering, and Medicine. (2017). *Seeing students learn science: Integrating assessment and instruction in the classroom.* Washington, DC: The National Academies Press.

National Research Council. (1996). *National Science Education Standards.* Washington, DC: The National Academies Press.

National Research Council. (2012). *A framework for K–12 science education: Practices, cross-cutting concepts, and core ideas.* Washington, DC: The National Academies Press.

Next Generation Science Standards (NGSS) Lead States. (2013). *Next Generation Science Standards: For states, by states.* Washington, DC: The National Academies Press.

Roehl, T. (2012). From witnessing to recording—material objects and the epistemic configuration of science classes. *Pedagogy, Culture, & Society, 20*(1), 49–70.

Schwarz, C. V., Passmore, C., & Reiser, B. J. (2017). *Helping students make sense of the world using Next Generation science and engineering practices.* Arlington, VA: NSTA Press.

Stroupe, D. (2014). Examining classroom science practice communities: How teachers and students negotiate epistemic agency and learn science-as-practice. *Science Education, 98,* 487–516.

Chapter Ten

An Innovative Approach to Improve College Readiness in Mathematics

A Collaborative Project

A. Susan Gay, Christopher W. Carter, and Carrie L. La Voy

Concern generated from recent measures of national and international mathematics achievement led the National Council of Teachers of Mathematics (NCTM) to produce *Catalyzing Change in High School Mathematics: Initiating Critical Conversations* (NCTM, 2018), which aims to focus the content and instructional practices in high schools to support the mathematics learning of every student. Years of conversation about students' lack of college readiness have resulted in the implementation of curriculum that is more rigorous and the use of accountability measures in high schools with the goal of more students graduating and being ready for college (Barnes et al., 2010).

Researchers (e.g., Barnes et al., 2010; McCormick & Lucas, 2011) have called attention to a lack of relationship between meeting graduation requirements for a high school diploma and preparedness for postsecondary education. Recent national data from ACT mathematics scores indicated that fewer than 50 percent of US high school graduates were ready for college-level mathematics coursework (ACT, Inc., 2017). This lack of preparation for success in postsecondary mathematics has merited the attention of those working in high schools, community colleges, and universities (e.g., Mesa et al., 2014; NCTM, 2018).

Local districts and their mathematics teachers have considered what changes may address the same nationally identified needs for high school mathematics success and preparation for postsecondary coursework. Chris Carter, a chapter author who is a graduate student and a high school mathematics teacher in a growing suburban school district, noticed that some high school seniors at his school were not ready for College Algebra at a community college or university. Chris worked with his two coauthors, mathematics teacher educators, to develop a classroom-based research project to modify an existing course, Algebra 3/Trig, to become Senior Algebra.

District mathematics specialists and school administrators provided technological support. They also approved the course with its new curricular vision and innovative teaching practices aimed at addressing gaps in mathematical knowledge.

PLANNING AND DELIVERING THE SENIOR ALGEBRA COURSE

It was clear that this Senior Algebra course would require modifications that would make it different from a traditional mathematics class. The Algebra 2 teachers identified passing juniors who, in their judgment, did not have an adequate understanding of the concepts necessary to be successful in College Algebra. The teachers recommended that those students take Senior Algebra, which would address gaps in knowledge from Algebra 1 and Algebra 2.

Differentiation and Remediation

It soon became apparent that students in Senior Algebra had various misunderstandings and gaps in conceptual and procedural knowledge. Remediation was a fundamental element of the course design. Differentiation was used to ensure each student received guidance and support to develop mathematical understanding. One type was a weekly, individualized, student-driven learning activity. From a teacher-provided list of state content standards typically aligned with prior mathematics courses and deemed necessary for success in College Algebra (e.g., simplifying numerical and algebraic expressions and graphing on a coordinate plane), students selected what they were going to work on, created individualized goals, and developed a plan for how they would accomplish their goals. The planning was done during the week so that on Friday, the students could complete the work during the class period.

Students could work individually or collaboratively. Since students were encouraged to find their own resources to accomplish their individual goals, the teacher demonstrated search strategies and possible video websites as one type of accessible resource. At the end of the class period, students wrote a reflection on the learning and progress they made on the objective they had chosen. This activity was an excellent opportunity for students to identify their areas of strength and areas they needed to continue to address, to harness and hone individual study habits, and to discover available learning resources.

Throughout the school year, students determined their readiness for assessment and designed their own methods of demonstrating their understanding. For example, students could give a class presentation, create an instructional video, or take a teacher-designed assessment. Daily homework was assigned to the large group on most days of the week. The homework assignments utilized tiered practice problems. For each set, students attained a certain amount of points in order to receive full credit for the assignment, but they could make choices to meet their individual needs.

For example, a struggling student could complete problems in Level 1 of the assignment; these problems focused on remedial tasks and were worth one point each. Therefore, the student had to complete many of these problems in order to attain the number of points for full credit on an assignment. In contrast, a Level 3 problem, worth three points, asked a student to complete a more rigorous problem that challenged the student to build a deeper understanding. Students could choose problems from one or more levels and choose which problems in each level they would complete. This approach required students to self-assess while working at the level appropriate for them to enhance their knowledge and skills.

Extensive communication among us played a vital role during the fall semester of the school year. Chris wrote daily observations on the climate and culture of the classroom, including lesson success, student engagement, and assessment results. Susan and Carrie read and responded to these observations, creating discussions and generating new ideas that allowed us to constantly critique and modify various elements of the course. Most of these discussions were held electronically, although occasionally we met face to face.

Incorporating Students' Voices

While Chris wrote daily observational notes about students' reactions to class activities, it was also important to hear directly from all of the students. Students shared their thoughts, observations, and feelings in informal ways through regular class discussions. They also completed quarterly surveys. Likert scale items measured students' opinions and experience with elements of the course including lessons and projects completed in class, homework, and individualized activities. Others measured students' perceived value of the course for their future, as well as their opinions about the difficulty and pacing of the course. The remaining items surveyed students' enjoyment and asked them to assess the effort they were putting into the course. The survey also contained a set of four free response questions asking what they enjoyed about the class, what they would change about the class, to share memorable lessons and moments in the class, and to write any other comments or suggestions. Survey responses were discussed by the research team and used to influence changes in the course elements and methods of instruction.

Elements that students identified as unhelpful for their learning were removed or modified. For example, the process to create, complete, and assess the individualized remedial learning activity was adjusted several times throughout the school year. Elements of the course or lesson designs that students found helpful were enhanced and used more often; those included working in groups and using online resources and preferred formative assessments. Students recognized when these changes were being made and appreciated having influence. Because Chris was honest about the purpose of the surveys, students felt ownership in the course. Survey responses showed a noticeable increase in students' confidence and a perceived increase in their understanding of mathematical concepts. The students viewed the course activities as preparing them to be successful in future mathematics courses and working well with their learning styles. Many also shared that they enjoyed coming to class each day; no student withdrew.

TEAM MEMBERS' PERSPECTIVES

We independently reflected on this collaborative classroom-based research project. Commentary connects our ideas and experiences to work and observations from others. Carrie discusses how she benefited from this collaboration below. Because this was a new experience for her, she appreciated the mentoring she received as she learned from a colleague about how to support graduate students beyond the traditional classroom setting. She also valued the opportunity to work with a practicing K–12 teacher.

CARRIE'S REFLECTION

I feel fortunate to work with students who have strong content knowledge and are also passionate about teaching. I enjoy this dynamic, and every semester I learn something new. My students' enthusiasm for teaching inspires me to work harder and continue to evaluate my own strengths and weaknesses in the classroom. As a result of this experience, I learned new ways to support graduate students in different settings. This work was designed to fulfill requirements for a graduate course that did not come with a set curriculum but focused on specific outcomes related to the unique work setting of the graduate student. Initially, we spent a fair amount of time designing a learning experience that would benefit Mr. Carter both in his path to completing an advanced degree and also in growing as an educator. This setting was different from what we usually see in graduate education, with the overall experience feeling more collegial. As a team of three, we posed questions, gave feedback, and shared ideas. The learning goals were student driven yet directed and supported by the course instructors.

One thing that made the experience unique for me was the makeup of the team. Having one graduate student and two university faculty members gave us more perspectives to influence and enhance the work. Working with a colleague pushed me to think about how I could better mentor graduate students. Being relatively new to teaching in this type of individualized setting, I felt supported to complete my part of the work in the best way possible.

I am proud of the work we did in this course. I have enjoyed watching Mr. Carter grow from a preservice teacher to a practicing educator and graduate student. I appreciated this opportunity to work closely with someone who is teaching in the K–12 world. As a faculty member in higher education I worry that I will become disconnected from what happens in "the real world." I know my university students value teachers who stay connected to K–12 classrooms, and this experience helped me stay engaged with what happens in the field.

In her reflection, Carrie cites the project as an impactful learning experience and notes its collegiality. Researchers (e.g., Hartman, 2018; Lau & Stille, 2014; Yuan & Mak, 2016) have described the importance of parity among collaborators engaged in school and university research partnerships and indicate that roles can change during the process. While this project involved a classroom teacher who was a graduate student and two university faculty members (and thus parity was not truly possible), it was Chris who identified the need in his school and a way to address the need.

While often it is the university faculty members who control discussions with graduate student teachers (e.g., Smedley, 2001), which could include the choice of research topic, that was not the case here. In fact, as Chris developed innovative practices for the course, the role of the two teacher educators was to pose questions, offer adjustments, and provide encouragement. This working relationship aligned with experiences described by Yuan and Mak (2016) who researched "collaborative action research" (p. 382) where the university partner provided guidance and support and the school-teacher chose a research question and made the plan to implement and evaluate the changes to classroom practice. Among the benefits to university faculty in a participatory research environment, Lau and Stille (2014) mention better understanding of the reality of the classroom. Carrie realized this as a benefit to her as a teacher educator.

Reflection is a key component of action research. The university researcher may take a lead in encouraging the classroom teacher to develop reflective abilities and to use reflections to guide steps in the research process (Yuan & Mak, 2016). In addition, Goodnough (2010) describes how, as a university faculty member working with teachers in an action research community, she examined her own views about teaching during the action research process. In this project, Carrie also engaged in reflection about her professional growth and likely future responsibilities working with graduate students to support their classroom-based research.

Based on Chris's project, Susan made connections to what she had noticed among her own students. As a result, she researched further and implemented changes in her classroom.

SUSAN'S REFLECTION

During meetings at the beginning of this project, I listened to Mr. Carter talk about the needs of and choices made by some of the high school juniors and seniors taking mathematics courses at his school. His description generated some connections to what I had noticed about the students in my two mathematics content courses for elementary preservice teachers.

Some of my students, who had been in high school just two years prior to taking my courses, were less motivated to complete assignments, were more distracted by personal devices, and seemed to have less willingness to try than students in previous years. While it was reassuring to know that high school teachers were observing similar behavior, I had to acknowledge that these behaviors were more pervasive and not just related to future PK–5 teachers taking university mathematics courses.

These observations about the behavior of both groups of students resulted in an exploration of characteristics of Generation Z, those born beginning around 1995 (e.g., Seemiller & Grace, 2017). Generation Z includes my university students and the high school seniors in Mr. Carter's school at the time of this project.

The information I gathered led to rethinking some aspects of my courses to try to address needs. While I did not implement the same types of differentiated instruction done in the high school course, I did incorporate more choice in assignments, more online work that could be done at a time of each student's choosing during a given period, more video rather than lecture and print media only, and more interactive hands-on work during class time.

In her reflection, Susan notes that the Senior Algebra students and the preservice teachers, all members of Generation Z, have experienced an environment similar to that described by authors (e.g., Luke & Elkins, 1998; Rodriguez & Hallman, 2013) writing about the New Times associated with rapid changes in technology, communication, and communities. Generation Z is even more strongly connected to technology than Millennials; they have been surrounded by technology from birth (e.g., Geck, 2006; Seemiller & Grace, 2017). The technology they constantly use allows them to communicate and collaborate with others instantly regardless of where someone is located and to access the diverse amount of information available on the internet (Geck, 2006). As students, Generation Z values active engagement in learning activities (e.g., Mendoza, 2018; Schwieger & Ladwig, 2018). Mendoza's (2018) study of twelve general education college students in 2017 found that all of them wanted to be "doing something" (p. 115) when they described how they wanted to learn. Schwieger and Ladwig (2018) said Gen Z prefers "hands-on experience" (p. 51). Susan's decision to increase the interactive hands-on work in class aligns with the work of others that suggests this may be meeting the needs of her students.

Generation Z students are "observers" (Seemiller & Grace, 2017, p. 23), meaning that they first want to watch another person do a task correctly and then they are willing to try. This learning preference is manifested in students' interest in watching instructional videos (e.g., Pearson, 2018; Seemiller & Grace, 2017). Generation Z students are also characterized as being comfortable engaged in individual learning (e.g., Schwieger & Ladwig, 2018; Seemiller & Grace, 2017). They even prefer independent self-paced learning, such as "completing an online module or watching an instructional video" (Seemiller & Grace, 2017, p. 23).

Susan's choice to include more videos as instructional resources on course content and more online work aligns with the interest her students likely have for observing others doing relevant tasks, self-pacing, and learning independently. One of the key features of the Senior Algebra course emphasized student responsibility for learning; students made independent choices about what they needed to learn, located learning resources on their own, and managed their own pace of learning. These features in both courses align with what research suggests is a learning preference for Generation Z.

Below, Chris reflects on how this experience affected his work as a teacher. He writes about the value of collaboration and the importance of reflection in his own practice. His commitment to students is evident as he highlights the importance of student feedback and opportunities for reflection in his current classroom.

CHRIS'S REFLECTION

This project has been one of the most influential experiences I have had. To collaboratively develop and teach this course was unlike anything I have done in the realm of education. We were all stakeholders, working together for the benefit of students. Reflection and feedback are elements that had the greatest impact on my teaching philosophy. During this project, I made it a point to ask my students regularly to critique the course, both formally through quarterly surveys and informally through guided class discussions. These informal discussions were rooted in a variety of questions: If they were the teacher, what would they change? What would they keep? What was too easy? What was too challenging? Do they feel more confident in their math skills? Are they more confident in themselves? I believe that by having these conversations, the students felt a stronger sense of value in my classroom, which positively affected my classroom's culture. Based on feedback, I modified the course to better suit students' needs. Before this project, I never gave my students this kind of voice. Perhaps, as a young educator, I was scared to hear the critiques from my students. However, I have learned that the benefits of this information far outweigh any potential disappointment I may feel.

In addition to utilizing student feedback, I still use a number of the remediation tools I developed while working on this project. I was introduced to these differentiation strategies in a graduate course taught by Dr. La Voy, so it was cool to implement them under her guidance. For example, tiered practice problems are still a staple in my assignment arsenal. Almost all of my students need remedial instruction occasionally. Having a number of differentiation techniques in my teaching toolbox has proven to be immensely helpful. I also have a newfound appreciation for collaboration between professional educators. Having multiple minds question and critique my lesson plans and classroom choices yielded what I would say to be incredible results.

In his reflection, Chris describes his view of the collaborative nature of the working relationship he had with the teacher educators and a district curriculum coordinator who supported the work to develop the Senior Algebra course. He perceived an openness during the interactions, which is a goal of university-school research partnerships (e.g., Lau & Stille, 2014; Yuan & Mak, 2016). He describes the relationship as coming close to the goal of parity, an element in the research process described by Lau and Stille (2014) where team members share equally and respect each other's strengths and contributions.

This project began with a school-based problem identified by the classroom teacher that was related to increasing students' college readiness; all of the steps taken were in furtherance of addressing that problem. This is not always the case in collaborative school-university research. Hartman (2018) notes, "[p]ractitioners focus on solving problems of practice to increase student learning" (p. 619); thus, their ideas are not always valued when decisions are made about a research focus. Because the project did address a problem of his choice, Chris has an increased sense of empowerment related to achieving a professional goal which, as others (e.g., Goodnough, 2010; Lau & Stille, 2014) noted, can be one very positive outcome of school-based collaborative research.

In other mathematics classes he teaches, Chris mentions continuing use of some differentiation strategies used in Senior Algebra. Research (e.g., Subban, 2006) has acknowledged the benefits of implementing differentiated instructional practices in today's classrooms. Tiering is commonly associated with effective differentiation (Tomlinson, 2017). This student-centered practice supports all students in meeting established learning goals in a manner that allows them to work with a variety of appropriately challenging and individualized tasks (Tomlinson & Imbeau, 2010). In differentiated classrooms, learning experiences are purposefully designed to meet a variety of needs. In this setting, student choice is essential; teachers work to provide "appropriately challenging learning experiences for all their students" (Tomlinson, 2017, p. 8). Research (e.g., Parker et al., 2017; Tomlinson, 2017) suggests student choice can enhance learning and increase engagement and motivation in the classroom.

As the most impactful aspect of the experience, Chris mentions the value of reflection and feedback. He notes the questions he asked regularly in class to gather feedback and the more formal written surveys that were used to be sure that everyone had the opportunity to provide feedback. The use of questionnaires to elicit student feedback on courses is common in universities (e.g., Richardson, 2005), but may be less so in high schools. The surveys were formulated to gather information that was specific to some of the new elements in the course and students' perceived value and engagement. Asking questions that address elements where feedback can be helpful gives the instructor the opportunity to make quick adjustments in teaching that will address students' concerns (Lewis, 2001). As Lewis (2001) noted, when feedback is gathered, it is important to respond to the students, letting them know what was learned from the information they provided and what changes, if any, will result.

THE POWER OF MENTOR CONVERSATIONS

It can be difficult to be open to receiving student feedback, especially as a relatively new teacher. In this class, the use of the feedback surveys early and periodically in the school year and Chris's willingness to make adjustments to the course activities in response to the feedback was indeed a likely factor in the feelings of students' investment in the class success, their own success, and the sense of community in the class. Goodnough (2010) notes that teachers are taking a risk when they engage in research. Chris described this risk when he talked about asking his students for feedback and then being willing to make changes based on that feedback. He also took a risk at the beginning of this project by taking a lead to teach the new course with innovative features that had the potential to address an identified problem of lack of college readiness.

Risk-taking involves imagination as teachers select, implement, and test new teaching practices they expect can support students in their classrooms

(Goodnough, 2010). In the process, teachers can change their views of themselves and their ways of teaching (Goodnough, 2010). Chris notes his increased confidence and professional growth. He also talks about how the knowledge acquired from this project has shaped his teaching in general. After the project, we shared reenergized feelings about our individual work responsibilities. Through the project experiences, Chris expanded his instructional repertoire of strategies and grew in the ability to be reflective about his teaching. Both teacher educators gained new connections to a real-world school setting and saw ideas that were part of graduate courses and mentor conversations come to life in a classroom. These experiences provided new motivation to continue to teach.

REFERENCES

ACT, Inc. (2017). *The condition of college & career readiness 2017.* Retrieved from https://www.act.org/content/dam/act/unsecured/documents/cccr2017/CCCR_National_2017.pdf

Barnes, W., Slate, J. R., & Rojas-LeBouef, A. (2010). College-readiness and academic preparedness: The same concepts? *Current Issues in Education, 13*(4). Retrieved from https://cie.asu.edu/ojs/index.php/cieatasu/article/view/678/56

Geck, C. (2006). The Generation Z connection: Teaching information literacy to the newest net generation. *Teacher Librarian, 33*(3), 19–23.

Goodnough, K. (2010). The role of action research in transforming teacher identity: Modes of belonging and ecological perspectives. *Educational Action Research, 18,* 167–182.

Hartman, J. J. (2018). Urban school district-university research collaboration: Challenges and strategies for success. *Education and Urban Society, 50,* 617–640. doi: 10.1177/0013124517713611

Lau, S. M. C., & Stille, S. (2014). Participatory research with teachers: Toward a pragmatic and dynamic view of equity and parity in research relationships. *European Journal of Teacher Education, 37,* 156–170. http://dx.doi.org/10.1080/02619768.2014.882313

Lewis, K. G. (2001). Using midsemester student feedback and responding to it. *New Directions for Teaching and Learning, 2001*(87), 33–44. doi: 10.1002/tl.26

Luke, A., & Elkins, J. (1998). Reinventing literacy in "New Times." *Journal of Adolescent & Adult Literacy, 42,* 4–7.

McCormick, N. J., & Lucas, M. S. (2011). Exploring mathematics college readiness in the United States. *Current Issues in Education, 14*(1). Retrieved from http://cie.asu.edu/ojs/index.php/cieatasu/article/view/680

Mendoza, K. R. (2018). *Engaging Generation Z: A case study on motivating the post-millennial traditional college student in the classroom* (10821906) [Doctoral dissertation, San Diego Christian College]. Retrieved from ProQuest.

Mesa, V., Wladis, C., & Watkins, L. (2014). Research problems in community college mathematics education: Testing the boundaries of K–12 research. *Journal for Research in Mathematics Education, 45,* 173–192.

National Council of Teachers of Mathematics (NCTM). (2018). *Catalyzing change in high school mathematics: Initiating critical conversations.* Reston, VA: Author.

Parker, F., Novak, J., & Bartell, T. (2017). To engage students, give them meaningful choices in the classroom. *Phi Delta Kappan, 99*(2), 37–41.

Pearson. (2018). Beyond millennials: The next generation of learners. Retrieved from https://www.pearson.com/content/dam/one-dot-com/one-dot-com/global/Files/news/news-annoucements/2018/The-Next-Generation-of-Learners_final.pdf

Richardson, J. T. E. (2005). Instruments for obtaining student feedback: A review of the literature. *Assessment & Evaluation in Higher Education, 30,* 387–415.

Rodriguez, T. L., & Hallman, H. L. (2013). Millennial teacher: A storied landscape of diversity in "New Times." *Multicultural Perspectives, 15*(2), 65–72.

Schwieger, D., & Ladwig, C. (2018). Reaching and retaining the next generation: Adapting to the expectations of Gen Z in the classroom. *Information Systems Education Journal, 16*(3), 45–54.

Seemiller, C., & Grace, M. (2017). Generation Z: Educating and engaging the next generation of students. *About Campus, 22*(3), 21–26. https://doi.org/10.1002/abc.21293

Smedley, L. (2001). Impediments to partnership: A literature review of school-university links. *Teachers and Teaching, 7*, 189–209. https://doi.org/10.1080/13540600120054973

Subban, P. (2006). Differentiated instruction: A research basis. *International Education Journal, 7*, 935–947.

Tomlinson, C. A. (2017). *How to differentiate instruction in academically diverse classrooms* (3rd ed.). Alexandria, VA: Association for Supervision and Curriculum Development.

Tomlinson, C. A., & Imbeau, M. B. (2010). *Leading and managing a differentiated classroom.* Alexandria, VA: Association for Supervision and Curriculum Development.

Yuan, R., & Mak, P. (2016). Navigating the challenges arising from university-school collaborative action research. *English Language Teaching, 70*, 382–391. doi:10.1093/elt/ccw017

Chapter Eleven

Using Digital Spaces to Foster and Sustain an Informal Professional Learning Community

Joe O'Brien, Brian Bechard, Kori Green, and Nick Lawrence

Online professional learning communities represent a vibrant means for teachers to learn about, experiment with, and assess the pedagogical validity of emerging technologies. Participation arises from teachers' perceived strong sense of technology self-efficacy, which is a significant factor in willingness to integrate technology into instruction (Drossel et al., 2017), and from a belief in the importance of collaboration in the use of technology (Eickelmann 2011; Fraillon et al., 2014). This chapter explores how we three beginning teachers in separate school districts, in collaboration with our former academic advisor, used our experiences in two informal online professional learning networks (PLNs) not simply to persist but to thrive in digital and class environments where change was our only constant.

We first contextualize how Brian's, Kori's, and Nick's entry into the profession roughly coincided with the popularization of social media and the founding of companies such as Facebook (2004) and YouTube (2005). We then focus on the creation of an informal learning community and our collaboration with Joe, our former academic advisor, to inform a year-long online project between our students in two Kansas school districts and one in New York City. As our sense of technological self-efficacy increased, we emerged as leaders in a professional organization and migrated to a second PLN with a different purpose and larger membership. The chapter examines these two types of PLNs and implications for fostering persistence among beginning teachers.

POPULARIZATION OF SOCIAL MEDIA

Kori, Nick, and Brian graduated from the same university and entered the teaching force at the same time. Each of us entered the classroom just as the number of users exploded on several prominent social media platforms. In the 1980s, users initiated early forms of social media, such as Bulletin Board System, which provided an online meeting place, and CompuServe, which permitted file sharing. The dawn of the twenty-first century, however, is when the public witnessed the inauguration of sites such as Friendster (2002) and MySpace (2003). The latter sites permitted social networking, particularly among users who shared a common interest.

While MySpace ultimately attracted three million users, the broadening of Facebook's user base from college-aged students to the general public in 2006 truly opened online social networking to all facets of society. In turn, beginning in 2005 YouTube served as a platform for user-generated videos, while the inauguration of sites such as Weebly and Wix in 2006 enabled users to create their own websites. Finally, the launching of Twitter (2006), and later Instagram (2010) and Snapchat (2011) illustrated the ease of re-sharing. By the time we were readying for our first jobs in 2008, 39 percent of teens had shared what they had produced and 27 percent had created their own webpage (Lenhart et al., 2007). These figures rose considerably by 2018, when 85 percent of adolescents reported using YouTube and about 70 percent reported using Instagram and Snapchat (Anderson & Jiang, 2018).

Several features of social media caught our attention. First, these platforms meant that physical geography became irrelevant; they permitted users to create and sustain global, collaborative networked publics capable of acting civically (Davis & Jurgenson, 2014). Such publics are digital spaces resulting from the networked technologies where an "imagined collective . . . emerges as a result of the intersection of people, technology, and practice" (Boyd, 2010, p. 39). No longer bound by four walls, we realized the potential of a digital classroom as a networked public that connected students across multiple schools.

Second, the ability to better seek out and act on one's interests distinguishes one's engagement in a face-to-face public and one's social engagement in digital spaces (Ito et al., 2013). Creating a digital classroom, for example, enlarged the class size from twenty-five to up to one hundred students, enhancing the likelihood of engaging with peers of similar interests. Third, users are able to access an abundance of information and use digital tools to shape and express ideas in multiple ways unlike any time in the past, illustrating a shift from people as consumers of information to producers of knowledge. For us, this shifted the focus from us as purveyors of knowledge to our students acting on their interests and creating their own knowledge.

Fourth, (re)sharing one's self and ideas illustrates a dynamic, generative relationship between individuals, online information, and networked publics (Skoric et al., 2016). As evidenced by Twitter's transformation into a political forum, such sharing of user-generated knowledge offered us an opportunity to help our students "turn their self-expression into a form of public participation" (Rheingold, 2008, 101).

Finally, as witnessed by the advent of terms such as "on-demand" and "streaming," social media promote a sense of personal agency by allowing users to make decisions about their environment from matters as simple as what to watch to immersing themselves in digital worlds (Kumpulainen & Sefton-Green, 2014). Given our mission to prepare our students for life in a pluralistic, democratic society, we recognized how social media enabled us to offer our students unparalleled online democratic experiences, particularly in exercising their public voice.

CREATION OF A STUDENT PEER-TO-PEER ONLINE LIMITED PUBLIC NETWORK

The convergence of digital technologies leading to the popularization of social media generated a professional opportunity for us. Even as novice teachers, we experimented with technology, such as Kori's students creating History Shorts that were two-minute videos about historic events. One of Nick's early endeavors presaged our future direction. Given how his eighth graders struggled with engaging in face-to-face discussion without being distracted by each other's nonverbal communication, Nick experimented with and researched the use of intraclass online discussions. Doing so allowed his students to focus on what their peers were posting rather than on how they were visually reacting.

Sharing an interest both in technology and in middle school students, whom Brian describes as "weird, awkward, and fun," we initiated a discussion in 2010 that resulted in the Just War website. We created and piloted the Just War site on a social networking platform called Ning to offer our students an opportunity to cultivate their online public voices (Levine, 2008) by trying to influence their peers' thinking about war, a critical public policy matter.

The site, which served as an online limited public network open only to students in one of the three or four schools that shared roughly the same face-to-face class meeting time, allowed our middle school students to engage in interschool, synchronous deliberations about what justified war. Each online deliberation was embedded in a three-day lesson, where on day one students worked in small, face-to-face groups to respond to a prompt that then was shared on the Just War site with their digital peers from two or three other schools.

On day two, students read and responded to the initial group posts, which prompted a series of multiple, synchronous peer-to-peer (P2P) discussion threads during which students continually demonstrated a sense of personal agency, as is discussed later. Prior to logging off, each student posted a final thought about the discussion, usually prompted by a compelling question tied to the discussion topic. The students' posts then were summarized and used as part of the debriefing in the face-to-face classrooms on day three.

Students typically participated in seven or eight such discussions during the school year, with the final one devoted to a simulation of a United Nations (UN) Security Council meeting. Two features characterized the UN online discussion. First, students applied what they learned during the year to a contemporary war-related issue, such as the Syrian civil war or the Russian annexation of the Crimea. Second, adults assumed the role of UN Security Council members, logging on from places such as Great Britain and Washington State.

While the prior deliberations were designed as P2P discussions, this was the first and only time that adults participated, which raised the stakes for students to exercise their public voice (O'Brien et al., 2014). The endeavor was as complex as it seems, given how we needed to address technical, logistical, and pedagogical concerns (Lund, 2004), requiring much collaboration and a willingness to court the inevitable glitches. The features of, the actions undertaken, and the roles adopted in our online professional learning space align with the research on why teachers persevere, which offers a possible recipe for fostering teacher perseverance, particularly among early-career teachers.

EMERGENCE OF THE ONLINE PLN

While the P2P Just War online limited public network served as the group's primary focus, unknowingly a PLN, that is, a "system of interpersonal connections and resources" that can be used for informal learning, collaboration and exchange of knowledge and ideas (Trust, 2012, p. 133), gradually evolved. Changing membership and the continual adaptation to emerging technologies reflect the PLN's dynamic quality. While we initiated the Just War Project with Joe, teachers from different states also participated, including an urban Kansas teacher, a teacher from northern Virginia, and another from Upstate New York. Further, the project engaged a doctoral student who assisted with research for four years. The PLN also adopted and discarded several digital tools, such as Today's Meet and Vimeo, and migrated the entire project from the Ning platform to Schoology.

While the dynamics occurring in online professional learning spaces is understudied, research indicates that such spaces are characterized by "teacher inquiry leading to development [and collegial sharing] of projects that are sensitive to local context," where all participants are given room to make contributions and "agency to respond to local needs" (Tondeur et al., 2016, p. 116). Given this, not surprisingly, Nick especially recognizes that what keeps him going in this profession are the people who surround him, often in digital spaces.

In digital spaces, teachers support each other as "providers of feedback; modelers of practice; supporters of reflection; agents of relationships; agents of socialization; and, advocates of the practical" (Kelly & Antonio, 2016, p. 140). These researchers noted that "modelling of teaching practice, reflection on practice or feedback about practice" (p. 146) are atypical. In contrast, the PLN's core members wove practice, research, and theory so closely as to become inseparable.

Beginning with piloting the design of the initial Ning site and related instructional material, which were grounded in Lund's work (2004) and the then scant research on online, synchronous P2P discussions among middle school students, to later analyzing students' thinking through the lens of principles grounded in just war theory and adapting instructional material accordingly, the network's members constantly reflected upon their students, the Just War site, and their practice. Only in stepping aside and perceiving the group's collective efforts as a professional learning space did questions arise about our technological self-efficacy and about the group's persistence both within the context of the Just War Project and beyond.

SELF-EFFICACY IN THE ONLINE PLN

Our creation of the Just War site not only proved "difficult" but also demonstrated "the conviction and confidence which enable[d] them to prepare lessons involving the use of ICT [information and communications technology]," a sign of our technology self-efficacy (Drossel et al., 2017, p. 568). During our collaboration on the Just War site, a sense of collective self-efficacy seemed to coalesce as our efforts illustrated a belief in our ability to pursue relatively uncharted pedagogical territory related to P2P online synchronous discussions sequenced across a curriculum (Goddard et al., 2004; Ross & Gray, 2006). Our commitment to a P2P approach also showcased the importance we placed upon teacher-student relationships, a factor in teacher persistence. Our informal PLN was characterized by traits related to the fostering of collective self-efficacy and teacher persistence, such as shared decision making (Goddard et al., 2004), a willingness to engage in interschool activities (Ross & Gray, 2006), the opportunity for professional learning, and collaborative undertakings (Blasé, 2009).

Not surprisingly, teachers' ICT self-efficacy represents the most influential factor on use of technology. Buchanan, Prescott, Schuck, and Aubusson (2013) noted how opportunities for professional learning and engaging with peers in ways that enhanced their self-efficacy seemed critical to teachers remaining in the classroom. In the context of a PLN, though, one also needs to consider the importance of collective self-efficacy not only in engendering greater individual self-efficacy but also in how participation in the network empowers users to engage in shared decision making about furthering the collective goals. The following scenario illustrates how the dynamics of both the Just War site and our PLN fostered the students' public voice and sense of agency.

REFLECTING ON THE CASE OF THE PURPLE SQUIRREL

The case of the purple squirrel illustrates one way in which students' public voice and sense of agency were fostered through the Just War project. Prior to participating in the online discussions, each student chose an image to use as an avatar. One particularly vocal and articulate student, who proved quite adept at questioning and even challenging other students' posts, chose a purple squirrel image.

During one monthly discussion, we noted how several of the students' face-to-face peers also had adopted a purple squirrel avatar and how the "purple squirrels" seemed to collectively engage with a group of online peers from another school. While not antagonistic, the faux purple squirrels seemed both to academically defend and to socially protect the original purple squirrel, their face-to-face peer.

Given how the research suggested that youth disliked adult intervention in online P2P discussions, we decided to allow students to academically facilitate their own discussions, with mediation when needed. During the discussion, messages on Today's Meet flew among us as we sought to understand how and why this new dynamic was unfolding. We entertained questions such as why several face-to-face peers came to the aid of the purple squirrel; what this meant for the academic quality of the deliberation; what possible implications of this interaction existed for implementing an online limited public network; and where was the line between healthy online academic dialogue and cyberbullying.

Facing these questions, we first examined the online transcript from the day's discussion and the one from the prior month to explore what transpired digitally. After this review, we reconsidered and rearticulated the online discussion norms for the students, identified and implemented more thoughtful ways for students to pose replies, and explored ways to encourage students to connect digitally with peers from other schools. Through this process, we realized how the "free-flowing, organic use of social media" (Prestridge et al., 2019, p. 2) vividly illustrated key components of a PLN identified earlier, particularly the ones related to feedback and reflection on practice that Kelly and Antonio (2016) indicated teachers implemented the least (p. 140).

The case of the purple squirrel illustrates but one vignette arising from the group's experience with the Just War project. As we realized the benefits of our students' online learning experience, we sought to exercise our "public" or professional voice. We began to pursue professional opportunities—for example, collaboratively presenting about the project at national conferences—and moved from a more localized, limited public network directly connected to our classrooms to a more nationally focused PLN tied to a national professional organization, as discussed next.

TRANSITIONING FROM A STUDENT-ORIENTED PLN TO A PEER-ORIENTED PLN

The research suggests that the first five to six years is a pivotal period for teachers because many struggle with deciding whether to stay or to go (Lavigne, 2014). Not surprisingly, between 2015 and 2019, all three of us have grappled with this professional decision. One teacher shifted to an administrative position in his school, while a second one moved to a middle school in another district. Kori, although later than the others, just moved to a high school in a different district. While contemplating our professional futures, we found ourselves continuing with our current PLN but also helping to invigorate a related but very distinct second one. Beginning in 2013, we became regular presenters for the Technology Community at the National Council for the Social Studies (NCSS) annual conference. Starting in 2014, we assumed informal leadership roles in the Technology Community.

As with the Just War PLN, the NCSS Technology Community's active membership has consisted of a core group of educators with a rotating body of second-tier members. The core group consists of five classroom teachers, a school administrator, and two college professors, although recent events suggest the addition of two more classroom teachers. The second tier are five to seven educators who fairly routinely participate in several tech-related events during the year.

While one of the three teachers from the Just War PLN has stepped forward to coordinate the group's efforts, the position is more of a first among equals than a leadership position. Eventually, the highly active members began to exhibit PLN features such as shared decision making, collaborative endeavors, sensitivity to context, and the creation and execution of collective goals. As a PLN coalesced, the opportunity for the three teachers to foster change in NCSS in several ways also emerged.

STRIVING FOR AN ONLINE COMMUNITY OF CHANGE AGENTS

Drawing on the collective self-efficacy fostered in the Just War PLN, we hope to harness the power of a PLN and cultivate change in how NCSS approaches professional learning and collaboration in several ways. First, in concert with our Technology Community peers, we are moving beyond the one and done model of professional development to a more sustained approach to professional learning.

The PLN is designing a series of professional learning experiences across several platforms that offer users background on emerging technologies; opportunities to engage with experts such as those with a start-up app company or Google; time to experiment with the technologies; and a chance to digitally share experience and examples of their use of the technologies. Ultimately, the Technology Community is designing a blended model that incorporates face-to-face experiences, such as in the conference's tech lounge, and digital ones such as Twitter chats and webinars, which is more effective than either a strictly face-to-face or digital approach (Macià & García, 2016).

Second, we are transferring what we learned about forming and implementing collective goals in the Just War PLN to the one of our peers. In fostering students' public voice in the Just War network, for example, we encouraged students to use multiple features of social media, such as posting material online, engaging in an online text-based deliberation, and recording and uploading videos in real time. These features added a dynamic quality to the students' discussions, one enhanced by our reflection upon the students' thinking as revealed in the discussion transcript and the debriefing of each deliberation based on that reflection.

The most visible demonstration of how we took these lessons to heart in the Technology Community PLN was the recent adoption of a position statement on Youth, Media, and Digital Civic Engagement. Instead of merely posting the position statement online, this PLN intends to engage NCSS members in a dialogue about ways to operationalize the statement and to enable users to post material reflective of the statement's principles and recommendations. Doing so aligns with the effort to modify how NCSS delivers professional learning experiences.

Third, we are seeking to broaden our collaborative relations beyond full-time school or college-based educators to those in the technology field. Initially, the PLN formed relations with start-up companies such as ReCap and The Lamp by incorporating them into our series of face-to-face and online professional learning experiences. Now, the PLN is seeking to establish relations with Google. The members are realizing that as their goals, interests, and needs change, the nature of the PLN must adapt accordingly.

PLNS AS INCUBATORS OF PERSEVERANCE

By happenstance, our collaboration on a largely student-driven online project evolved into a PLN, one whose attributes complemented what the research suggested, enabled beginning teachers to persevere. Freedman and Appleman (2009) posited that those who persist possess a sense of purpose and self-efficacy, reflect upon their practice, are provided agency to influence change, and receive ongoing collegial support. Kori best captured these facets of perseverance: "I appreciate the challenge [of teaching]. It's a career that allows for change and innovation . . . to share [content] with students . . . see what other educators are doing in their classrooms [which] inspires me to see what I can do [with this] opportunity for growth."

Particularly for early-career teachers, formation of professional relationships, especially ones where they as beginning teachers are able to assume the role of an expert (Lavigne, 2014), helps both to engender a sense of resiliency and professional belonging and to affirm the value of their contributions. While the PLN seemed to emerge naturally, we made several conscious decisions that likely created the conditions for a PLN.

First, each member of the professional learning space sought to create a community of learners, one devoted to P2P collaboration in the pursuit of learning. While seemingly a simplistic idea, such thinking meant they envisioned a physical classroom as but one space in which their students might learn. This harks back to Nick's experience with the use of online intraclass discussions. At first blush, the thought of his students talking with each other via a computer when they were sitting next to each other seemed absurd. Now, such a notion seems no stranger than two friends sitting next to each other in silence as they rapidly send text messages to a host of other friends not physically with them.

The challenge for us became how to make the most of digital and face-to-face means to best foster multiple communities of learners. The manner in which a handful of students socially rallied behind the "purple squirrel" in her quest to question academically what another handful of students were posting, and were given the public space to do so, offers testimony to the educators' commitment to a community of learners. In joining the Technology Community PLN, the focus on community shifted from one of students to that of educators. Just as many of our peers reached the five- to six-year mark and decided to leave the profession, we deepened our commitment to it.

Second, rather than inoculating ourselves against the challenge of integrating ever-emerging technologies into our pedagogical repertoire, we purposefully embraced the challenge. Unquestionably, the opportunity for members in both PLNs continually to model for each other and to reflect upon their practice both aids in addressing this challenge and illustrates the dynamic, even "organic" nature of a PLN. Each monthly teleconference, for example, is peppered with side conversations on a member's use of a new technology. Finally, we chose to collaborate due to common interests and goals and then to share decision making, and to treat each other as equals, all features of social media in general and a PLN in particular.

While beginning teachers likely would view PLNs as daunting, we, along with Joe, created and engaged in one organically, and perhaps unknowingly, which resulted in leading middle school students to engage in high-quality online deliberations. Despite the fact that we possessed less than a decade of teaching experience when the Just War project began, our peers at national conferences often expressed amazement at what their students accomplished during the Just War discussions. At least for the three of us, participating in a PLN served as an incubator for perseverance in the classroom and now seemingly is serving a similar purpose persisting within the profession.

REFERENCES

Anderson, M., & Jiang, J. (2018). Teens, social media & technology 2018. Pew Research Center. https://www.pewresearch.org/internet/2018/05/31/teens-social-media-technology-2018/

Blasé, J. (2009). The role of mentors of preservice and inservice teachers. In L. Saha & A. Dworkin (Eds.), *International handbook of research on teachers and teaching* (pp. 171–181). London: Springer.

Boyd, D. (2010). Social network sites as networked publics: Affordances, dynamics, and implications. In Z. Papacharissi (Ed.), *A networked self: Identity, community, and culture on social network sites* (pp. 39–58). New York, NY: Routledge.

Buchanan, J., Prescott, A., Schuck, S., Aubusson, P., Burke, P., & Louviere, J. (2013). Teacher retention and attrition: Views of early career teachers. *Australian Journal of Teacher Education, 38*(3), n3.

Davis, J. L., & Jurgenson, N. (2014). Context collaps: Theorizing context colusions and collisions. *Information, Communication & Society, 17*(4), 476–485.

Drossel, K., Eickelmann, B., & Gerick, J. (2017). Predictors of teachers' use of ICT in school—the relevance of school characteristics, teachers' attitudes and teacher collaboration. *Education and Information Technologies, 22*(2), 551–573.

Eickelmann, B. (2011). Supportive and hindering factors to a sustainable implementation of ICT in schools. *Journal for Educational Research Online/Journal für Bildungsforschung Online, 3*(1), 75–103.

Fraillon, J., Ainley, J., Schulz, W., Friedman, T., & Gebhardt, E. (2014). *Preparing for life in a digital age: The IEA International Computer and Information Literacy Study international report.* New York, NY: Springer.

Freedman, S. W., & Appleman, D. (2009). "In It for the Long Haul"—How teacher education can contribute to teacher retention in high-poverty, urban schools. *Journal of Teacher Education, 60*(3), 323–337.

Goddard, R. D., LoGerfo, L., and Hoy, W. K. (2004). High school accountability: The role of perceived collective efficacy. *Educational Policy, 18*(3), 403–425.

Ito, M., Gutiérrez, K., Livingstone, S., Penuel, B., Rhodes, J., Salen, K., Schor, J., Sefton-Green, J., & Watkins, S. C. (2013). *Connected learning: An agenda for research and design.* Irvine, CA: Digital Media and Learning Research Hub.

Kelly, N., & Antonio, A. (2016). Teacher peer support in social network sites. *Teaching and Teacher Education, 56*, 138–149.

Kumpulainen, K., & Sefton-Green, J. (2014). What is connected learning and how to research it? *International Journal of Learning and Media, 4*(2), 7–18.

Lavigne, A. L. (2014). Beginning teachers who stay: Beliefs about students. *Teaching and Teacher Education, 39*, 31–43.

Lenhart, A., Madden, M., Macgill, A. R., & Smith, A. W. (2007). *Teens and social media: The use of social media gains a greater foothold in teen life as they embrace the conversational nature of interactive online media.* Washington, DC: Pew Internet & American Life Project.

Levine, P. (2008). A public voice for youth: The audience problem in digital media and civic education. In W. L. Bennett (Ed.), *Civic life online: Learning how digital media can engage youth* (pp. 119–138). Cambridge, MA: MIT Press. doi: 10.1162/dmal.9780262524827.119

Lund, K. (2004). Human support in CSCL: What, for whom and by whom? In J. W. Strijbos, P. A. Kirshner, & R. L. Martens (Eds.), *What we know about CSCL and implementing it in higher education* (vol. 3, pp. 167–198). Norwell, MA: Kluwer Academic Publishers.

Macià, M., & García, I. (2016). Informal online communities and networks as a source of teacher professional development: A review. *Teaching and Teacher Education, 55*, 291–307.

O'Brien, J., Ellsworth, T. M., Barker, T. W., Lawrence, N., Green, K., & Bechard, B. (2014). Online synchronous discussions, middle school students and mock UN Security Council. In W. Russell (Ed.), *Digital social studies* (pp. 197–216). Charlotte, NC: Information Age Publishing.

Prestridge, S., Tondeur, J., & Ottenbreit-Leftwich, A. (2019): Insights from ICT-expert teachers about the design of educational practice: The learning opportunities of social media. *Technology, Pedagogy and Education, 28*(2), 157–172.

Rheingold, H. (2008). Using participatory media and public voice to encourage civic engagement. In L. Bennett (Ed.), *Civic life online: Learning how digital media can engage youth* (pp. 97–118). Cambridge, MA: MIT Press.

Ross, J. A., & Gray, P. (2006). Transformational leadership and teacher commitment to organizational values: The mediating effects of collective teacher efficacy. *School Effectiveness and School Improvement, 17*(2), 179–199.

Skoric, M. M., Zhu, Q., Goh, D., & Pang, N. (2016). Social media and citizen engagement: A meta-analytic review. *New Media & Society, 18*(9), 1817–1839.

Tondeur, J., Forkosh-Baruch, A., Prestridge, S., Albion, P., & Edirisinghe, S. (2016). Responding to challenges in teacher professional development for ICT integration in education. *Educational Technology and Society, 19*(3), 110–120.

Trust, T. (2012). Professional learning networks designed for teacher learning. *Journal of Digital Learning in Teacher Education, 28*(4), 133–138.

Chapter Twelve

Hope as the Catalyst to Thrive in the Profession

Elizabeth Yomantas and Sarah Rosenthal

The purposes and aims of education have been debated for centuries. While the considerations of how to educate students and for what purpose are not new theoretical or practical questions, the world is ever changing. Now, the world is contextualized in New Times, where the competition is fierce and there is an emphasis and reliance on technology (Gee et al., 1996). Under fast capitalism, competition is found on a local and global scale. There is an increased divide between the rich and the poor, and there is a "winner takes all" mentality in this science and technology driven world situated in competition (Gee et al., 1996).

Schools are not immune from the challenges of New Times. As society changes, the fabric of teaching and learning in schools change. Furthermore, the roles of the teacher and the student change. While there are new ways of acting, talking, thinking, valuing, and being in the workplace as a result of fast capitalism, newly empowered educators cannot question the goals, values, and parameters of the new work order. There is both a demand and pressure to "keep up" and move faster, work harder, and maintain flexibility (Gee, 2000; Gee, 2004).

In this "fast capitalism" (Luke & Elkins, 1998, p. 5) that has invaded schools, teachers must respond to these demands. For example, teachers must foster collaboration, not for the purpose of human flourishing, but to develop communication skills that can then be applied under the new work order. Classrooms become centered on consumers and markets; moreover, teachers face pressure to make curricular decisions that prepare students for "an increasingly volatile and uncertain job market" (Luke & Elkins, 1998, p. 6).

Teachers and teacher educators must attend to the needs of the students under New Times while striving to promote equity and inclusion in both the explicit and implicit curriculum, uphold state curricular standards, and meet the multiple needs of all stakeholders involved in education. Teacher educators must, as Luke (2004) suggested, develop "transcultural and cosmopolitan teacher[s]" (p. 1438) through attending to generational ethos (Rodriguez & Hallman, 2013).

These challenges in education are both overwhelming and exhausting. Despite the interconnectivity of society, these challenges are often met in isolation and loneliness (Dussault et al., 1999). New Times has the potential to further dehumanize educators (Shapiro, 2010) and deskill the teaching profession (Tye et al., 2010). With an emphasis on consumers and markets even in the classroom, teachers may lose autonomy and creativity; they are expected to shapeshift with the new working order.

Exhausted from the demands of New Times, we individually searched for something to restore humanity back into the profession. We yearned for someone to share the tireless journey alongside. In this chapter, we explain how hope has propelled us from a posture of surviving into a position of thriving through a professional development school (PDS) partnership. We first share our stories of how personal experiences helped us examine what mattered in our teaching before discussing how the PDS contributes to our continuing professional development.

SARAH'S STORY

In 2015, at the age of thirty-six, I was shocked by a breast cancer diagnosis. This life-changing event created a break in my professional life. It took almost a year to complete six rounds of chemotherapy and four operations. Returning to teaching after almost a full school year of treatment and healing made me look at the meaning and purpose of what I did completely differently.

Teaching had become a grind and education felt transactional; I was no longer willing to continue working, isolated in a classroom, without defining what it was I wanted to accomplish. It was at this point that I was asked to mentor a teacher candidate from Pepperdine University. My teacher candidate, Davina Morales, was young, excited, and full of energy. Davina asked interesting questions, made quality suggestions to improve our lessons based on her learning, and reinvigorated my teaching. Collaborating with Davina inspired a new purpose and fostered new hope for my work as a teacher educator.

ELIZABETH'S STORY

In 2016, I made the transition from classroom teacher to teacher educator. I was eager to work alongside preservice teachers because of the hope and possibility they bring to the future of the collective work in the field of education. Part of my new position was to serve as the director of clinical practice. In this role, I worked alongside mentor teachers and administrators to secure student teaching placements and then support all stakeholders throughout the experience.

As I began working with mentors and administrators from various districts, I struggled to make connections and found schools to view beginning teachers as a burden rather than an opportunity. It seemed to be all about business and not about relationship. I learned that mentor teachers were often handcuffed by the overwhelming demands of their school sites, and so consequently, having a student teacher was just "one more thing."

SARAH AND ELIZABETH'S STORY

When Davina, a teacher candidate, was placed in Sarah's classroom by Elizabeth's predecessor, Elizabeth simply went to meet Sarah and provide her with an orientation so she was equipped to serve as a mentor teacher. Elizabeth did not expect anything extraordinary to come of this meeting; orienting mentor teachers was a regular part of her job. However, when Elizabeth met Sarah for the first time, she thought there was something different about her—she sensed goodness, calmness, and kindness.

Although Elizabeth often felt as if her presence is a burden for time-strapped mentor teachers, Sarah graciously extended the gift of time. She made Elizabeth feel welcome and important. As they talked, Elizabeth began to share her dream of developing a professional development school where candidates could learn the pedagogical aspects of becoming a teacher while also reimagining a humanized education in a safe and supportive environment.

Without hesitation, Sarah agreed to become a school partner. Unexpectedly, Elizabeth had found the coauthor of her dream. After their initial meeting, Sarah went to work to make this dream a reality. She was able to schedule a meeting with the executive director/principal, assistant principal, and HR director to talk about the potential partnership. At a school of nearly three thousand students, arranging a meeting with administrators was Sarah's first feat. Together, we presented the PDS plan to the administration team, and much to our surprise, we were offered full support.

GROWING HOPE

Critical literacy skills are required in order to respond to New Times in ways that preserve humanity in both the curriculum and lived experiences of the educational community (Luke & Elkins, 1998; Gee et al., 1996). If literacy is not limited to text forms and can be a way of "reading the world" (Freire, 1985), lived critical literacy in education responds to New Times with "thought, critique, and struggle" (Gee et al., 1996, p. 154) in the everyday actions of educators.

In the popular children's book *What Do You Do with an Idea?*, Yamada (2014) suggested that ideas must be cared for, protected, and relentlessly given attention. In the same way, hope must be given care, protection, and attention amidst the complex realities created within New Times. If not, hope runs the risk of disappearing and being replaced with cynicism, apathy, or disenchantment. According to Freire (1985), one of the tasks of the progressive educator is to unveil hope, no matter what the obstacles may be. There are challenges to growing and sustaining hope; as Freire notes, there is a continual connection between struggle and hope.

Hope is actively grown through the PDS partnership between Pepperdine University and Palisades Charter High School (PCHS). This PDS is rooted in a shared orientation and motivation of hope, and is nurtured through care, protection, and attention. The following section provides a short overview of what a PDS is and then explains how hope continues to grow through reclaiming a culture of excellence in our work, embodiment of educational theory, healing in personal and professional identities, and reimagining the future of education through the collective work.

GROWING HOPE THROUGH THE PDS FRAMEWORK

Cosenza & Buchanan (2018) define a PDSs as "collaborative learning environments which support the training of new teachers, provide professional development to mentor teachers, and make a commitment to student success through the process" (p. 3). PDS models have a history dating back to the late nineteenth century and were modeled on the medical school structure (Cosenza & Buchanan, 2018, p. 4). They were popularized across the United States around the year 2000.

The National Association of Professional Development Schools (NAPDS) states that there are nine essential elements that all PDS sites should have. Important aspects of the nine essentials include a comprehensive and unique mission statement; a shared commitment to the preparation of future educators; ongoing professional development and reflection; clear communication; and shared leadership, resources, and research (NAPDS, 2008).

The literature also explains the many challenges and complexities associated with the PDS model (Dana, 2017; Parker et al., 2016). Some of these challenges include threats to traditional institutional practices, complexities that arise when merging with two different school cultures, a lack of institutional financial support, and changes in educational policy that affect the partnerships (Darling-Hammond, 2005).

One of the aspects of the PDS framework is that there should be mutual benefits for all stakeholders (Sikma et al., 2018). The phrase *mutual benefits* connotes images of a transaction or trade in alignment with the values of New Times; however, a PDS should be more than this. Grain and colleagues (2019) conducted a research study to understand which aspects of an international service learning partnership are connected with the impact they have on the community. They found that friendships and relationships for social change were a core component of the partnerships' success. PDS partnership is built upon this same principle of friendship and social change.

An aspect of the work in this PDS is to bridge the public/private dichotomy in an effort to illuminate the human experience. Teacher candidates and mentor teachers have engaged in personal hobbies outside of school together. For example, PCHS is near the beach, so teacher candidates have gone surfing with mentor teachers before the start of the school day. Teacher candidates and mentor teachers have had open conversations about their personal faith, family relationship struggles, and challenges with mental health.

Additionally, we not only talk with each other about the PDS but also share about the personal aspects of our lives. Through these authentic relationships, New Times are challenged and hope in the work is restored. The literature does not indicate that hope is an explicit part of all PDS relationships or suggest that relationships in a PDS should extend beyond the professional and into the personal. However, in this particular PDS, a shared vision and friendship built through individual hope are the cornerstone of the collective work.

GROWING HOPE FROM SURVIVING TO THRIVING

Hope is grown through efforts to reclaim a culture of excellence in our work. A common and regular event in teacher preparation programs is the process of matching teacher candidates with mentor teachers through securing clinical placements. To secure a clinical placement, the university first had to ensure there are memoranda of understanding on file with the district, which is followed by a principal connecting student teachers with willing mentors.

This structure does not account for relationship building or a partnership built on shared personal interests or educational philosophies.

This process felt like "surviving" rather than "thriving," so we began to wonder how we could make the matching process and the semester-long experience more personalized. First, we decided that it would be important for mentor teachers at PCHS to apply to serve rather than be selected or assigned at random. This created a more level playing field and demystified the process of how to host a student teacher. PCHS values equity and openness—not only with students, but with faculty procedures as well. By establishing an application and interview protocol, the PDS was illuminated and it gained greater visibility on campus. This process benefited the teacher candidates as well. When they learned that their mentors had to apply, interview, and be selected in order to serve, they desired to invest fully in the experience; they know their mentors are quite committed to their success.

Teacher candidates felt more comfortable at PCHS before the first day of school. Because they had met several of the mentor teachers and had been oriented to the campus, they were more confident on the first day. The interview protocol served them well because soon after their experience at PCHS, the teacher candidates graduate and apply for teaching positions. This process is intimidating, and so the PDS interview allowed for candidates to gain interview experience in a low-stakes context.

The PDS has also shaped the onboarding process at PCHS for all teachers, not just teacher candidates. As new teachers and teacher candidates attended meetings together, a bond was created. They received professional development about promoting equity in the classroom, how to promote student engagement, co-teaching strategies, and more. This allowed everyone the chance to receive the tools they needed to thrive and the knowledge that they were not alone.

Veteran teachers began to see their value through the eyes of a future teacher; new teachers were supported in their dreams, and a culture of mutual respect and professional growth has taken hold. Mentor teacher Negin Mahmoudi (2019) stated:

> Being a mentor teacher was one of the most rewarding experiences of my professional career. I had the honor of witnessing, and playing a role in the development of, a student teacher who grew tremendously through processes of inquiry, trial and error, and meaningful reflection. Engaging in this work with my student teacher gave me a renewed sense of hope for the future of this profession.

Hope propelled us from surviving to thriving as we heal in our personal and professional identities. Educators are exhausted from isolation and a lack of togetherness in the field (Carr, 2018; Dussault et al., 1999). On an individual level, we faced regular doubts as to whether we are good enough to do the work we do in professional spaces. Understanding that many educators experience these feelings of doubt as well, we were inspired to provide spaces and places for the mentor teachers to feel that their role in supporting the PDS is critical.

Beyond the selection and pairing process, we wanted to breathe hope into the semester by regularly honoring the mentor teachers. Hosting a teacher candidate each and every day for a semester or the entire academic year is a large commitment; moreover, it is important to find ways to honor the willingness to mentor, the process of pairing, and the mentor teachers' commitment to equipping the next generation of educators.

In the process of becoming a mentor, the veteran teachers who hold themselves to a high standard are honored. The mentor teachers are given a voice in the PDS. For example, the suggestion to interview the teacher candidates before committing to hosting a student teacher came from a mentor teacher. Mentor teachers are also honored by a special program at the end of the year. During this time, all members of the PDS community are invited to a luncheon to honor the mentor teachers.

They are gifted with a mentor teacher certificate, PCHS attire, Pepperdine swag, and a succulent plant. The purpose of the succulent connects with the C. S. Lewis (2009) quote "The task of the modern educator is not to cut down jungles, but to irrigate deserts." We thank the mentor teachers for helping to irrigate deserts in the minds and hearts of the teacher candidates, and to help nurture hope into the future of the profession.

In addition to these gifts, the teacher candidates prepare a written speech that they read in front of the PDS community. The speech they prepare responds to the prompt "How did your mentor teacher help you grow as an educator?" The PDS community is reminded that together, our collective work can make the world better. This kind of recognition is the difference between surviving and thriving; it remains a rarity at the average public school.

The spirit of hope has propelled the PDS from surviving to thriving in the way PCHS embodies educational theory. We developed a unique vision for teacher candidates at the inception of the PDS; we yearned for the PDS to be a place where teacher candidates can see educational theories come to life and discover how they play out in concrete, tangible, and complex ways.

In this case, PCHS is a place where educational theory is embodied in complex, multidimensional, concrete forms. PCHS is a school where students come from over one hundred zip codes, and the school openly states its mission of equity and excellence in education. Equity in education takes places in numerous tangible ways on the school campus. The teacher candidates get holistic exposure to what the daily pursuit of equity in education looks like, and they get to see the struggle and hope of living out the theories they learned in their education coursework.

Students are exposed to the process of selecting and implementing diverse curricula; making accommodations for students with exceptional needs; inclusive practices for the new landscape of gender; the ability to dialogue across different ethnic, racial, social, and cultural backgrounds; and the opportunity to learn from administration as they navigate complex terrains.

Teacher candidates gain this exposure in multiple ways. In addition to PCHS hosting teacher candidates, PCHS also hosts Pepperdine students who are in introductory education courses as a precursor to the student teaching experience. In these observational periods, Pepperdine students visit a variety of mentor teachers' classrooms, attend field trips hosted by the PCHS administration, and learn from the campus unification director. During the student teaching experience, teacher candidates are included in the new teacher mentor meetings hosted at PCHS, often focused on exploring complex issues of equity at the school.

Sarah serves as a critical link between the teacher candidates and PCHS issues in equity. When issues arise at PCHS, teacher candidates often let Elizabeth know. Elizabeth relays the information to Sarah, and together, we brainstorm how to support the teacher candidates in unpacking the complex issues.

The students see the daily pursuit of equity in education across multiple plains as they participate in this PDS. These theories in coursework feel as though hope is surviving; however, seeing this struggle in real-time action allows hope to thrive and redefine the future of education.

Hope allows us to reimagine the future of education through collective work. We share resources on our campuses. For example, we presented at the Southern California Professional Development School (SCPDS) conference that was held at Pepperdine University in March 2019. The keynote speaker, Dr. Trudy Arriaga, presented on her book titled *Opening Doors: An Implementation Template for Cultural Proficiency* (2016).

After the session, Sarah brought the book and the concepts back to PCHS. For the 2019–2020 academic school year, the entire PCHS community adopted the text as the school year framework. The school leadership revised their teacher observation template to focus on issues of equity to better serve the students at PCHS. As a result, the Pepperdine students are also coached on how to teach from an equitable framework so all students have access to the curriculum.

The PDS is a quiet revolution. It is a decision to reject mediocrity and embrace hope. This partnership has not only inspired hope on both school sites but also brings hope to the future of education. Teachers who graduate from PDS training also are more likely to become change agents in the schools where they teach. For example, teacher candidate Kelly Peterson stated:

From my time at the PDS, I developed my leadership skills and educational experiences under the guidance of my professors and mentor teachers. I was pushed out of my comfort zone to lead the class in takeover, taught how to create engaging lesson plans, and praised for improving my classroom management. My mentor teachers challenged, advised, and celebrated me through my growing experiences. My academic development in my education program and my student teaching at my placement have prepared me for my future classroom. My time in the PDS has sparked my aspiration of becoming a teacher who impacts my students to be lifelong learners.

SUSTAINING HOPE

Hope must be continually pursued through the PDS partnership in an effort to continually resist the negative aspects of New Times. PDSs can serve as a third space in which "academic, school-based, and community-based knowledge come together in less hierarchical and haphazard ways to support teacher learning" (Zeichner et al., 2015, p. 124). This PDS thrives on the dreams of all stakeholders/participants and consequently seeing them come to fruition.

We are not the only authors or definers of hope. When asked to reflect on her experiences in the PDS, Pepperdine teacher candidate Christina Haug explained that her hope came from the PCHS community's investment in her. Even under New Times, Christina was seen as a human being rather than a product. Despite the growing connections between business and education (Gee et al., 1996), Christina was seen in her full humanity, and therefore, she is learning to extend this gift to her students.

CHRISTINA'S STORY

When you're twenty-two, and a part-time student teacher and part-time college student, it's hard not to feel like there's something missing. You spend your days trying to help students figure out who they are, and show them love enough to make them love themselves. You spend your days trying to be enough of an outsider as a student to be a good teacher, and enough of an outsider as a teacher to be a good student—but enough of an insider to do both well. You spend your days trying to master a subject while also trying to remember and process everything about today and also trying to remember and process the lessons you learned through high school memories yesterday. You spend your days trying to figure out how to do everything, and do it well, and be an instrument of goodness and purpose in the world.

So, when you're twenty-two and a part-time student teacher and a part-time college student, it's hard not to feel like the whole world rests on your shoulders. Because every morning, you wake up and find that you're still twenty-two, and you don't know who you are and are just now learning how to love yourself. And every morning, you wake up wondering where the insider and outsider boundaries are, and if you'll ever belong fully as a student or teacher ever again. And every morning, you wake up wondering if anyone could ever truly master a subject, and if today is more important than yesterday or the other way around. And every morning, you wake up and the bell rings and you look into your eleventh grade class's eyes and you feel that same hurt and callousness that they feel because, after all, you're only twenty-two and yesterday wasn't long enough ago to fill the holes that high school left in your heart. And so you spend your day wondering how on earth you can be an instrument of goodness and purpose in the world because—for the first time—you realize that other people's yesterdays and todays and tomorrows sort of depend on you . . . and you're only twenty-two.

But then you get to know your mentor teacher, a lady like Ms. Saiza, who understands the Freirean idea that teaching is well-defined capacity to love. She gives students minty gum if they fall asleep in first period and apologizes that they have to get up so early to catch the bus. She gives you opportunities to teach, and lets you do it your own way, and backs you up when you mess up without even having to ask her. She tells you that you're a natural educator, and that it's not about who you are, it's about what you believe in, and that relationships are the most important thing, and that in the end "it's just high school," and it will do more good than evil, regardless.

And one day, you wake up and the bell rings and you look into the students' eyes and you see yourself for the first time—a twenty-two-year-old who knows what she believes in and therefore, who she is—a student and a teacher, in community, with love—fully both, fully connected, forever trying to squeeze the lessons out of the whispers of today, and the songs of yesterday, and the dreams of tomorrow. And on that day, you've never been happier to be a student teacher, learning and teaching and growing courageously, because you realize that maybe the only thing you'd been missing were people who believed in you—the rest you had carried with you all along.

This PDS resists Gee's notion that "you *are* your projects" (2000, p. 413) under New Times. While the concept of "shape-shifting portfolio people" is a dominating cultural trend, we resist the idea that this project defines who we are, and we believe the partnership is worth far more than merely a résumé item. Rather, because this project is based on the cornerstone of friendship and is rooted in hope, the collaborative work is an extension of who we are and who we strive to be as human beings.

In the future, the PDS partnership continues to strive to cultivate hope for all participants. In upcoming future projects including a mental health wellness center at PCHS and further investments in equity across both campuses, this partnership will continue to strive for these aspects of hope in our collective work that both propels the PDS community from surviving to thriving and helps all stakeholders to reimagine the future of education.

It is a dream that this PDS utilizes the concrete reality (Freire, 1972) not merely as a space to robotically deliver curriculum and face the challenges of New Times with fear and exhaustion. Rather, it is a shared dream that the PDS will continue to pursue hope together in our teaching and learning landscapes in order to transform both the current PDS community and the future of education.

REFERENCES

Carr, T. (2018). *Joy in teaching: Build resilience, fight burnout, reclaim joy: A research-based framework of action for educators*. Mount Vernon, IA: Throw Out the Box, LLC.

Cosenza, M., & Buchanan, M. (2018). A short history of professional development schools: Looking backward and forward. In M. Buchanan & M. Cosenza (Eds.), *Visions from professional development school partners: Connecting professional development and clinical practice* (pp. 3–10). Charlotte, NC: Information Age Publishing.

Dana, N. (2017). Practitioner inquiry and PDS work: A reflection on 25 years of purpose, problems and potential. *School-University Partnerships: Teacher Inquiry, 10*(4), 5–12.

Darling-Hammond, L. (2005). *Professional development schools: Schools for developing a profession*. New York, NY: Teachers College Press.

Dussault, M., Deaudelin, C., Royer, N., & Loiselle, J. (1999). Professional isolation and occupational stress in teachers. *Psychological Reports, 84*(3), 943–946.

Freire, P. (1972). *Pedagogy of the oppressed* (2nd ed.). New York, NY: Herder and Herder.

Freire, P. (1985). Reading the world and reading the word: An interview with Paulo Freire. *Language Arts, 62*(1), 15–21.

Gee, J. (2000). Teenagers in new times: A new literacy studies perspective. *Journal of Adolescent & Adult Literacy, 43*(5), 412–420.

Gee, J. P. (2004). *Situated language and learning: A critique of traditional schooling*. London: Routledge.

Gee, J., Hull, G., & Lankshear, C. (1996). *The new work order: Behind the language of the new capitalism*. Boulder, CO: Westview Press.

Grain, K., Katumba, T., Kirumira, D., Nakasiita, R., Nakayenga, S., Nankya, E., Nteza, V., & Ssegawa, M. (2019). Co-constructing knowledge in Uganda: Host community conceptions of relationships in international service learning. *Journal of Experiential Education, 42*(1), 22–36.

Lewis, C. S. (2009). The abolition of man, or, reflections on education with special reference to the teaching of English in the upper forms of schools [e-book]. HarperCollins E-Books.

Luke, A. (2004). Teaching after the market: From commodity to cosmopolitan. *Teachers College Record, 106*(1), 1422–1433.

Luke, A., & Elkins, J. (1998). Reinventing literacy in "New Times." *Journal of Adolescent & Adult Literacy, 42*(1), 4–7.

Mahmoudi, N. (2019). Personal communication, October 8.

National Association of Professional Development Schools (NAPDS). (2008). *What it means to be a professional development school* [policy statement]. Columbia, SC: Author. Retrieved from https://napds.org/nine-essentials/

Parker, A., Parsons, S., Groth, L., & Brown, E. (2016). Pathways to partnership: A developmental framework for building PDS relationships. *School-University Partnerships, 9*(3), 34–48.

Rodriguez, T., & Hallman, H. (2013). Millennial teacher: A storied landscape of diversity in "new times." *Multicultural Perspectives, 15*(2), 65–72.

Shapiro, S. (2010). Revisiting the teachers' lounge: Reflections on emotional experience and teacher identity. *Teaching and Teacher Education, 26*(3), 616–621.

Sikma, L., Dikkers, A. G., & Lewis, S. (2018). Introduction to the themed issue: Furthering the education profession: Partnerships in action. *School-University Partnerships: Furthering the Education Profession, 11*(4), 1–4.

Tye, D., Tye, K., & Tye, B. (2010). The slow death of the American teacher. *Obama and Education, 5*(1), 31–37.

Yamada, K. (2014). *What do you do with an idea?* Seattle, WA: Compendium Inc.

Zeichner, K., Payne, K., & Brayko, K. (2015). Democratizing teacher education. *Journal of Teacher Education, 66*(2), 122–135. https://doi.org/10.1177/0022487114560908

Index

academic inequity, 116
achievement debt, xiii
action research, 125
activist ally, 4, 10
agentive identities, 3, 7, 58, 102
alternative pathways, ix, 73
Adequate Yearly Progress (AYP), 82, 84, 86, 99

charter schools, 29, 43, 69, 71, 74, 76–77, 90
chronology, 55, 56, 58, 61, 65
College and Career Readiness Standards, 16
Common Core State Standards, 16, 86, 88, 95
community of practice, 94, 100, 103
cosmopolitan teachers, 146
counterstories, 10, 58
critical consciousness, 15, 17, 20–21, 98
critical inquiry stance, 95, 101, 103
critical literacy, 83, 94, 97, 100, 148
cultural competence, vii, xiii
culturally relevant teaching, xiii, 4, 84
culturally responsive teaching practices, xiii, xiv, 41–42, 42, 44, 45, 46, 49
cultural studies, 94
culturally sustaining approaches, vii
curricular standards 146

dialogic, xviii, 17, 21

disciplinary landscape, xii, xvii
disciplinary innovation, xii

emergent bilingual, 15, 16–18, 19, 24
EngageNY, 94
English as a second language (ESL), xiv, 3, 5, 15, 19
English Language Arts (ELA), xiv, xvi, 3, 86, 88, 93–95, 99–100, 104
English Language Development (ELD), 5
English Language Learner (ELL), 3, 5, 15, 42, 47
entwined symbiosis, xiv, 42, 44–49
Every Student Succeeds Act (EESA), 16, 90

fast capitalism, 145
formative assessment, 124
Framework for K–12 Science Education, 110

Generation Z, 126–127

Hands across the World, 5, 9
High Schools That Work, 85
high-stakes testing, xiv–xv, 71, 82, 83, 90, 98–99

individualized education plan (IEP), 29
inquiry, 82, 89, 95, 97, 100, 103–104, 109
invested leaver, vii, x–xi, 10

invested stayer, ix–xi, xi, xvi, 3, 7, 10, 11, 27, 103

Just War, xvii, 135–142

landmark catalysts, viii, ix, xii, xvii
Lau vs. Nichols (1973), 16
linguistic appropriateness, 17
linguistically sustaining approaches, 17, 20–21, 24

monoglossic norms, 17
moral agents of change, 17, 24
multicultural education, 4
multilingual pedagogies, 17
multimodal, 104
mushfake, 8

National Association of Professional Development Schools (NAPDS), 148
National Council for Teachers of Mathematics (NCTM), 121
National Council for Social Studies (NCSS), 139, 140
National Science Education Standards, 110
native speaker, 17, 19
neoliberalism, xv, 69, 71
New Criticism, 97
New Times, 126, 145–146, 148–149, 153–154
Next Generation Science Standards (NGSS), xvii, 109–111, 114–116, 118
New York State modules, 94–95, 97
No Child Left Behind (NCLB), xiv, 82–85, 90, 95
neoliberal ideology, xv, 69–71, 99

peer-to-peer discussion (P2P), 135–136
professional development school (PDS), xvii, 59–60, 60, 84, 146, 147–149, 151–155
project-based learning (PBL), 4
political landscape, xii, xiv, 82
praxis, xiv, 15, 18, 22, 45
professional learning, xi, xii, xviii, 65, 78, 84, 112, 136, 137, 138, 140, 141
professional learning communities (PLC), xvii, 84, 91

professional learning networks (PLN), 133, 141–142

refugee, xiii–xiv, 3, 5–6, 9–10, 12
Research Practice Partnership (RPP), xvii, 112–113
resilience of teachers, viii, xi

scripted curriculum, 95, 97–98
shape-shifting portfolio people, 154
social justice, vii, 3–5, 6, 9, 12, 23, 27, 49, 56, 95, 98
social landscape, xii, 35
social studies education, 37, 69–70, 81, 88, 89, 91, 139
social justice pedagogy and socially just pedagogy, 4, 6, 9, 95
Southern California Professional Development Schools (SCPDS), 152
spheres of influence, xi, 28–29
standard English, 17, 19
standardization, 83, 86, 94, 98, 103

teacher attrition, ix–x, 69
teacher persistence, xviii, 137
teacher retention, viii, xi
teacher socialization, 55
teacher strike, 62–63, 81, 84
teacher unions, ix, 43, 55, 61–63, 73, 74–77
top-down educational mandates and reform, ix, xi, xv, 43, 65, 69, 83, 90, 95, 97, 98, 103
transculture, 146

Universal Design for Learning (UDL), 29
university-based teacher preparation, ix, 66
university–school research partnerships, 112, 128

Western New York Network of English Teachers (WNYNET), 93–100, 103
white gaze, 17
white privilege, 31, 35
white savior, 19, 43

Youth Voices Conference, 93–94, 96, 101–104

About the Contributors

Brian Bechard is a seventh grade social studies teacher at Mission Trail Middle School in Olathe, Kansas. He earned a BSE in secondary education and an MSE in curriculum and instruction from the University of Kansas, as well as an MS in instructional design and technology through Emporia State University. He has presented at national conferences and serves on the leadership team of the National Council for the Social Studies (NCSS) Technology Community. Brian's contact information is bbechardmt@olatheschools.org.

Deborah Bertlesman is a high school English teacher at Olmsted at Kensington in Buffalo Public Schools in Buffalo, New York, and a current officer and former president of the Western New York Network of English Teachers. She is a doctoral student at the University at Buffalo and former adjunct professor at Buffalo State College. Her research focuses on how to build and uphold networks of educators that advocate for high-quality, research-based practices in English language arts (ELA) classrooms with a specific interest on the interaction between urban education and neoliberal reform. She is dedicated to teaching students through inquiry processes centered on social justice. Her work has been presented at the National Council of Teachers of English (NCTE) and published in *English Journal*. She can be contacted at deborahbertlesman@gmail.com.

Hannah M. Britten graduated from Fitchburg State University with a BS in English and secondary education. She finished her practicum at Fitchburg High School and became a long-term substitute prior to graduation. She is currently the middle school English teacher at Holy Family Academy, a private school in Gardner, Massachusetts. Her recent accomplishments include a *Poetry of Protest* presentation for the 2019 New England Association of Teachers of English conference, an interactive teaching demonstration designed to offer teachers new ways of thinking about and using poetry; creating new clubs (such as a book club) and opportunities for deeper academic and civic engagement at her school; and beginning her MA in literature. Fascinated by stories, she aims to pass along not only the appropriate curricula but also a passion and hunger for the subject. She can be contacted at hanmbrit@gmail.com.

L. Lynn Stansberry Brusnahan is a professor at the University of St. Thomas in Minnesota, where she chairs the Department of Special Education. Lynn is coauthor of *Do Watch Listen Say: Social and Communication Intervention for Autism Spectrum Disorder*, was the 2012 Autism Society of America Professional of the Year, and has a PhD from the University of Wisconsin–Milwaukee in urban education. Lynn serves on the Council for Exceptional Children's (CEC) Division on Autism and Developmental Disabilities (DADD), and she is the parent of an adult with autism. She can be contacted at llstansberry@stthomas.edu.

Christopher W. Carter is a high school mathematics teacher at Olathe Northwest High School in Olathe, Kansas. He earned a BA in mathematics and an MSE in curriculum and instruction from the University of Kansas. A 2014 Kansas Teacher of Promise, he serves on multiple committees at the Kansas State Department of Education and is chair of the Kansas State Mathematics Standards Review Committee. He is currently pursuing a PhD in curriculum and instruction with an emphasis in mathematics education at the University of Kansas and can be contacted at ccarteronw@olatheschools.org.

Katharine Covino, an assistant professor of English Studies, teaches writing, literature, and teacher-preparation classes at Fitchburg State University. Her research interests include critical pedagogy, gender, and identity. Three areas of current scholarship focus on (1) examining the implications of including critical pedagogy in elementary literacy classrooms, (2) applying indigenous lenses to critically examine and retell cultural myths, and (3) exploring the disconnects that can arise for novice middle and secondary English teachers as they begin their teaching careers. Additionally, she has published and presented on a variety of issues related to literacy praxis, entwining theory and practice to support English teachers at all levels in their classrooms. Guided by her interest in promoting critical, collaborative, and reflective pedagogy, she has served for multiple years as a faculty mentor at Fitchburg State University. Prior to teaching at the university level, she taught middle school and high school in Austin, Texas. In addition to her work as a teacher, researcher, and mentor, she is also a children's book author with multiple upcoming projects. She can be reached at kcovinop@fitchburgstate.edu and at https://www.insanelyawesomephonebook.com.

Lauren Thoma Ergen is a teacher of multilingual learners, especially students with limited or interrupted formal education, at Apollo High School in Saint Cloud, Minnesota. She also teaches as an adjunct instructor at the College of Saint Benedict and Saint John's University. She earned a BA in English/communications arts, secondary education, and teaching English to speakers of other languages (TESOL) from the College of Saint Benedict and Saint John's University, and an MA in teaching English as a second language from Saint Cloud State University. Her recent research has focused on students with limited or interrupted formal education, social/emotional skills, and social justice pedagogy. Her work has appeared in *The European Educational Researcher*. She can be contacted at lauren.ergen@isd742.org.

Margaret Flynn is a middle school language and literature teacher in Denver Public Schools and a seventh/eighth grade language and literature curriculum lead and instructional leadership coach. She earned her BSE in Secondary English Education and ME in Curriculum and Instruction from the University of Kansas. Her work at the middle school level focuses on curating standards-aligned rigorous curriculum that includes differentiated resources and culturally relevant content to deeply engage all students in their learning. She strives to synthesize curriculum according to historical means, cultural integrity, and new era perspectives. She is dedicated to fostering inclusiveness, tolerance, and inquiry in her students. She has led professional development workshops across school campuses and presented to a team of educators from around the state of Colorado, speaking on how to plan an effective interdisciplinary unit for National History Day. She has been recognized as a distinguished teacher in Denver Public Schools since 2016. She can be contacted at mcflynn5@gmail.com.

Shelley Neilsen Gatti, PhD, is associate professor in special education at the University of St. Thomas. She completed her PhD in educational psychology at the University of Minnesota in 2001. She is a longtime member of CEC, CCBD, and DEC and served on various state and national boards. She has experience working with students with challenging behaviors in rural and urban settings. Since 2016, she has worked closely with St. Thomas's teacher residency programs in collaboration with Saint Paul Public Schools and Minneapolis Public Schools. Her areas of interest include teacher preparation and evaluation, schoolwide Positive Behavioral Interventions and Supports (PBIS), and assessment and intervention for students with challenging behavior. She can be contacted at slneilsengat@stthomas.edu.

A. Susan Gay is associate professor of mathematics education in the Department of Curriculum and Teaching and the Department of Mathematics at the University of Kansas. Her former positions include middle school mathematics teacher and mathematics specialist for the Oklahoma State Department of Education. Her recent research focuses on students' understanding of mathematical concepts and the instructional resources used by mathematics teachers and students. Her work has been featured in journals such as *International Journal of Research in Education and Science*, *Mathematics Teacher*, *Mathematics Teaching in the Middle School*, *Issues in the Undergraduate Mathematics Preparation of School Teachers*, and *PRIMUS: Problems, Resources, and Issues in Mathematics Undergraduate Studies*. She can be contacted at sgay@ku.edu.

Kori Green is a ninth grade world/tenth grade US history teacher at Wichita West High School. She earned a BA in history and women's studies and a BSE and MSE in secondary social studies at the University of Kansas. She is interested in the use of social media, has published in the *Journal of Education & Learning* and *The Social Studies*, presented at conferences at the national level, and serves on the Kansas Council for the Social Studies' board and the NCSS Technology Community's leadership team. Kori's contact information is kgreen6@usd259.net.

Candice Guy-Gaytán is assistant professor of science education at the University of Nevada–Reno. Her research focuses on the coordination of scientific practice and content in K–12 classrooms, with an emphasis on model-based reasoning and sensemaking. She explores this coordination through a variety of contexts including curriculum development and implementation in and out of schools and in preservice and in-service teacher education programs. Prior to joining the faculty at the University of Nevada–Reno, she completed a PhD in science education at the University of California–Davis and was a K–8 science specialist in San Francisco, California. She can be contacted at cgaytan@unr.edu.

Heidi L. Hallman is professor of curriculum and teaching in the Department of Curriculum and Teaching at the University of Kansas. Her research interests include how prospective teachers are prepared to teach in diverse school contexts and professional development opportunities for teachers. Hallman is the coauthor of *Secondary English Teacher Education in the United States* (2018), winner of the 2018 Richard A. Meade award for research in English education. She is also coauthor (with Melanie Burdick) of *Community Fieldwork in Teacher Education: Theory and Practice* (2015). Hallman's work has been published in *English Education, Teaching Education, Teacher Edu-*

cation Quarterly, *Equity & Excellence in Education*, *Journal of Adolescent & Adult Literacy*, *English Journal*, *Reflective Practice*, and *Multicultural Perspectives*, among others. She can be contacted at hhallman@ku.edu

Deeqaifrah Hussein is director of special education at Minneapolis Public Schools. She is also a mentor for preservice teachers at the University of St. Thomas. She is a community advocate and the vice president of Somali Parents Autism Network. Hussein has fifteen years of experience in education and has been licensed in general education as well as special education. Currently, she is pursuing her doctorate in educational leadership with a focus on autism. She is an active community advocate, an educator, and a parent of children with autism. As the first autism licensed Somali American teacher in Minnesota, she advocated and helped write a grant to increase the diversity of autism teachers in the state of Minnesota. She can be reached at Deeqaifrah.hussein@mpls.k12.mn.us.

Meghan A. Kessler is assistant professor of teacher education at the University of Illinois–Springfield. Her research interests include teacher education and evaluation, social studies education, and justice-oriented social studies teaching. She is particularly interested in teacher identity and development across the career spectrum and teachers' enactments of policy or reform. Her work has been published in *Teaching Education* with a forthcoming publication in *Teachers College Record*. Prior to pursuing her PhD in curriculum and instruction at the University of Illinois at Urbana-Champaign, Kessler taught middle and high school social studies for six years. She can be contacted at makessl2@uis.edu.

Carrie L. La Voy is a multiterm lecturer in the department of curriculum and teaching at the University of Kansas. She has experience teaching mathematics at many levels, including middle school, preschool, and college. She has presented about mathematics education at state, regional, and national conferences and serves as a board member for the Kansas Association of Teachers of Mathematics. She can be contacted at cll@ku.edu.

Nick Lawrence is an assistant principal at the East Bronx Academy for the Future, where he also taught eighth grade US history, remedial writing, German language, and college preparatory elective courses. He earned BSE and MSE degrees from the University of Kansas and has worked with nonprofit organizations and university faculty on the use of digital media. He has published in *The Social Studies* and the *Journal of Education and Learning* and has presented his work at national and international conferences. Nick's contact information is nicklawrence@eastbronxacademy.org.

Eric D. Moffa, EdD, is assistant professor of education studies at Washington and Lee University in Lexington, Virginia. He teaches courses in middle/secondary education and education policy. Prior to his professorship, Eric taught high school social studies in West Virginia for ten years. His research interests include rural education, citizenship education, and teaching controversial issues. His work has been published in various journals, including the *Rural Educator*, *Social Studies Research and Practice*, and *The Social Studies*. He can be contacted at moffae@wlu.edu.

Joe O'Brien is an associate professor in middle/secondary social studies education at the University of Kansas. He earned his doctorate at the University of Virginia, was on the faculty at Virginia Commonwealth University, and taught social studies in grades 7–12. His research interests include the instructional use of social media and historical thinking. Joe's contact information is jeobrien@ku.edu.

Martin Odima Jr. is a special education teacher and preservice teacher mentor in the Saint Paul Public School district in Minnesota. In addition, he is an adjunct faculty member in the department of special education at the University of St. Thomas. Martin received his bachelor's degree in psychology from the University of Minnesota and his academic behavioral strategist (ABS) license and a master's degree in special education from the University of St. Thomas. He has seven years of experience as a special education teacher. Martin has been recognized for his work in education from the Saint Paul Public School district and organizations such as Minnesota Educators for Excellence (E4E) and Advocates for Achievement (AFA). He has been a guest speaker on topics involving educational technology, diversity, and inclusive practices for students with disabilities at the University of St. Thomas, University of Minnesota, and University of Wisconsin–River Falls. He can be reached at martin.odima@spps.org.

Kristen Pastore-Capuana is assistant professor of English education at Buffalo State College, where she teaches undergraduate and graduate English language arts education courses and coordinates field experiences and community partnerships. A former high school English teacher in western New York, Pastore-Capuana's fourteen years of experience informs her work as a researcher and teacher educator. Her research interests include critical literacy pedagogy, secondary English language arts teacher development, and teacher development. She recently coedited (with Heidi Hallman and Donna Pasternak) two collections examining English language arts methods courses: *Using Tension as a Resource: New Visions in Teaching the English Language Methods Class* (Rowman & Littlefield, 2019) and *Possibilities, Challenges, and Changes in English Teacher Education Today: Exploring*

Identity and Professionalization (Rowman & Littlefield, 2019). She is also the assistant director of the Western New York Network of English Teachers (WNYNET—http://www.wnynet.org/). She can be contacted at pastorka@buffalostate.edu.

Arpan Patel is a high school social science teacher at Roberto Clemente Community Academy in Chicago, Illinois. He earned his BA in history with a minor in secondary education from the University of Illinois at Urbana-Champaign. As a former student and current instructor at Chicago Public Schools, Arpan's professional practice is dedicated to the advancement of educational justice in the city of Chicago through community-based participation and the power of collective labor action. Recently, Arpan was a member of the Chicago Teachers' Strike, advocating for equitable funding and resources for Chicago students and staff over the course of a work stoppage that lasted eleven days. He can be reached at apatel1792@gmail.com.

Toni M. Poling is an award-winning, national board certified, eleventh and twelfth grade English teacher at Fairmont Senior High School in West Virginia and an adjunct professor in the school of education, health, and human performance at Fairmont State University. She holds a BA in English and an MA in secondary education from West Virginia University, advanced credentials in advanced placement English, certification in public school administration, and is currently pursuing her EdD in curriculum, instruction, and assessment. Since being named 2017 West Virginia Teacher of the Year, Mrs. Poling has presented at professional development conferences at both the national and state level and serves as a contributing blogger for *Education Post*, the West Virginia Council of Teachers of English, and the National Network of State Teachers of the Year. Her recent focus has been on advocating for and elevating the teaching profession. Most recently, she was elected to the board of directors of the National Board for Professional Teaching Standards. She can be contacted at tmpoling@k12.wv.us.

Terri L. Rodriguez is professor of education at the College of St. Benedict and St. John's University and a former secondary English teacher. Her recent research focuses on teacher preparation for diversity, equity, and social justice. Her work has been featured in journals such as *English Education*, the *European Educational Researcher*, *Literacy Research and Instruction*, *Multicultural Perspectives*, *Linguistics and Education*, the *New Educator*, and *Teaching and Teacher Education*. She is coauthor of *Supporting Muslim Students: A Guide to Understanding the Diverse Issues of Today's Classrooms* (2017) published by Rowman & Littlefield. She can be contacted at trodriguez@csbsju.edu.

Sarah Rosenthal is an English teacher at Pacific Palisades Charter High School and also a coordinator of smaller learning communities, professional learning communities, and the professional development school partnership with Pepperdine University. Her recent focus has been on teacher preparation, mental health, and a commitment to social justice. She graduated with dual degrees in business administration and rhetoric from the University of California–Berkeley. She also has a master of arts degree in educational administration from California State University–Northridge. She can be contacted at srosenthal@palihigh.org.

Sylvia Scoggin is the secondary science curriculum facilitator for Washoe County School District in Reno, Nevada. A high school biology teacher for twenty-two years, she has presented at several national conferences and serves on the Science Coordination and Supervision Committee for the National Science Teaching Association (NSTA). She earned her BS in civil engineering at the University of Colorado and an MBA in international business at the University of Oregon. Sylvia can be contacted at sscoggin@washoeschools.net.

Leah Shepard-Carey is a PhD candidate in second language education at the University of Minnesota–Twin Cities. She teaches a variety of graduate and initial licensure courses related to English language education and world language education. Before her doctoral studies, she taught in early childhood bilingual and elementary and middle school–level English as an additional language settings. Leah's research interests focus on multilingual and culturally sustaining literacy instruction for young emergent bilinguals and critical approaches in teacher education. She has presented at numerous national and international conferences and her research has been featured in the *Journal of Early Childhood Literacy* and *Linguistics and Education*. She can be contacted at shepa090@umn.edu.

Allison J. Spenader is associate professor of education at the College of St. Benedict and St. John's University in Minnesota and a former K–12 ESL, EFL, and Foreign Languages (Swedish) teacher who has worked in the United States and internationally. She trains preservice teachers in both ESL and world language methods. Her research focuses on intercultural and language proficiency development in study-abroad, content-based approaches to world language education, and recently, social justice in world language and ESL education. She provides training for faculty and students on intercultural development and designs and leads study-abroad programs for university students in a variety of countries. Her research has been published in *Foreign Language Annals*, *Language Teaching Research*, and *Frontiers: The Interdisciplinary Journal of Study Abroad*. Allison has supported Minnesota language teachers by serving on the executive board of the Minnesota Council for the Teaching of Languages and Cultures for a decade, including as president. Allison can be contacted at aspenader@csbsju.edu.

Elizabeth Xeng de los Santos is assistant professor of secondary science education at the University of Nevada–Reno. Her research interests include teacher learning and professional development, science assessment, and organizational sensemaking in complex educational systems. Her work has been published in journals such as the *Journal of Research in Science Teaching* and featured in conferences such as the annual meetings of the *National Association for Research in Science Teaching* and *American Educational Research Association*. She received her PhD in curriculum, instruction, and teacher education from Michigan State University and taught for eleven years in public middle and high schools in Maryland and California. She can be reached by email at xdelossantos@unr.edu.

Elizabeth Yomantas is assistant professor in the teacher preparation program at Pepperdine University in Malibu, California. She also serves as the director of Professional Development Schools. Before earning a PhD in education from Chapman University, Elizabeth was a middle school English teacher. Her research interests include culturally responsive experiential education with preservice teachers, core reflection in teacher education, and indigenous Fijian schooling and epistemology. She can be contacted at elizabeth.yomantas@pepperdine.edu.

Garrett Zecker is a high school English teacher at Fitchburg High School in Fitchburg, Massachusetts, and an adjunct professor, writer, and actor. He earned his MA in English from Fitchburg State University and his MFA in fiction from the Mountainview MFA. His work at the high school level focuses on facilitating students' ownership of the classroom's approaches to literature and writing through community-based partnerships and creative service-learning projects that address the concerns his students recognize in the cultural, civic, and global identity of their time. Zecker's fiction has recently been accepted as a semifinalist of the 2020 Machigonne Fiction Contest, making him a member of the New Guard. His fiction and nonfiction have appeared most recently in *Black Dandy*, *Porridge Magazine*, *Assignment Magazine*, *Parhelion Literary Magazine*, and a wide variety of other publications. Links to his work, along with original essays and literature guides, can be found at http://www.garrettzecker.com. He can be contacted at mrzecker@gmail.com.

www.ingramcontent.com/pod-product-compliance
Lightning Source LLC
Chambersburg PA
CBHW030139240426
43672CB00005B/188